OUT OF

YOUR

CAVE

UNSTUCK

INTO

YOUR

CALL

MARK JOBE

MOODY PUBLISHERS

CHICAGO

All Scripture quotations, unless otherwise indicated, are taken from the Holy Bible, New International Version®, NIV®. Copyright © 1973, 1978, 1984, 2011 by Biblica, Inc.™ Used by permission of Zondervan. All rights reserved worldwide. www.zondervan.com. The "NIV" and "New International Version" are trademarks registered in the United States Patent and Trademark Office by Biblica, Inc.

Scripture quotations marked NASB are taken from the *New American Standard Bible*®, Copyright © 1960, 1962, 1963, 1968, 1971, 1972, 1973, 1975, 1977, 1995 by The Lockman Foundation. Used by permission. (www.Lockman.org)

Though the accounts related in this book are true, some names and minor details have been changed to protect privacy.

Edited by Brandon O'Brien
Interior design: Ragont Design
Author photo: Jennifer Coleson
Cover design: DogEared Design
Cover photo of cave copyright © 2012 by timnewman/iStock; of seated man's body copyright © 2008 by Imagine Golf/iStock; of seated man's head copyright © 2014 by OSTILL/iStock. All rights reserved.

Library of Congress Cataloging-in-Publication Data
Jobe, Mark.
  Unstuck : out of your cave into your call / Mark Jobe.
     pages cm
  Includes bibliographical references.
  ISBN 978-0-8024-1222-5
  1. Change (Psychology)—Religious aspects—Christianity. 2. Self-actualization (Psychology)—Religious aspects—Christianity. 3. Motivation (Psychology)—Religious aspects—Christianity. I. Title.
  BV4599.5.C44J63 2014
  248.4—dc23
                          2013051154

We hope you enjoy this book from Moody Publishers. Our goal is to provide high-quality, thought-provoking books and products that connect truth to your real needs and challenges. For more information on other books and products written and produced from a biblical perspective, go to www.moodypublishers.com or write to:

Moody Publishers
820 N. LaSalle Boulevard
Chicago, IL 60610

3 5 7 9 10 8 6 4

Printed in the United States of America

Everyone gets stuck spiritually. It doesn't matter if you are a brand-new Christian or a seasoned pastor, discouragement and stagnation will come. This is why I love *Unstuck*, because it works for the churchgoer and the church leader. Drawing from one of the most interesting stories in the Bible, *Unstuck* will help you see and love God in the middle of a crisis of faith.

> **—Darrin Patrick**
> Lead Pastor of The Journey, St. Louis, Vice President of Acts 29, chaplain to the St. Louis Cardinals, author of *The Dude's Guide to Manhood* and *Church Planter*, coauthor of *Replant*.

This is the story of a pastor whom God has used to help people who are "stuck" get up, and get on with their journey. As you read these pages you will be introduced to ministry in Chicago—raw, unpredictable and at times scary.

Mark is a leader, an innovator and risk taker. But also his heart for people shines through these pages, and he is well qualified to introduce people to the grace of God for hope and healing. You will be inspired, instructed, and encouraged to take some giant steps in your own life when you read this book!

> **—Erwin W. Lutzer**
> Senior Pastor of The Moody Church

Unstuck is the perfect book for helping people get free from all that holds us back and to get us moving toward God's very best. Mark Jobe brilliantly uses lessons from the life of the Old Testament prophet Elijah in *Unstuck* to help us discover God's greater purpose in our lives. We all get stuck, and when we do, we need *Unstuck!*

> **—Dave Ferguson**
> Lead Pastor of Community Christian Church, Spiritual Entrepreneur of the NewThing Network

In God's providence, I received this book as I was heading into a time-out to seek the Lord for fresh direction and wisdom for this season of my life and ministry. Having often found myself stuck in an emotional or spiritual cave over the years, I was both encouraged and challenged as I read *Unstuck*, and am grateful for the many timely, helpful insights from the life of His servant Elijah.

> **—Nancy Leigh DeMoss**
> Author, *Revive Our Hearts* radio teacher

My friend and co-laborer for the gospel in Chicago, Mark Jobe, takes readers on a powerful journey of real, biblical change through the life of Elijah. Read this engaging resource to get unstuck from despair and live the life God plans for you for His glory.

> **—James MacDonald**
> Senior Pastor of Harvest Bible Chapel, author of *When Life Is Hard* and *Vertical Church*.

God has blessed Mark Jobe with a vision as big as the city of Chicago, where he leads a growing community of dynamic churches. Drawing lessons from the life of the prophet Elijah and using captivating stories to illustrate biblical truth, Jobe shows how to get unstuck and get involved in what God is doing in the world.

> **—Dr. Philip G. Ryken**
> President of Wheaton College

Biblical, relevant, refreshing, and from someone I know has spiritual reality and maturity. We can all learn from such people.

> **—Dr. George Verwer**
> Founder of Operation Mobilisation

Whether you are stuck in a snowdrift, stuck in a long line when you are late for your plane, or just stuck in an insoluble problem, being stuck is annoying. But when you are stuck spiritually it is more than annoying—it is dangerous! When your walk with Jesus is stagnant and uninspiring, count on it: Satan will be there to offer you something more exciting. Thanks to Mark Jobe, you don't need to stay stuck. Mark offers us a ton of great advice in this book about how to get spiritually unstuck. Read it and enjoy a newfound freedom in Christ!

—Dr. Joseph M. Stowell
President of Cornerstone University

Thank God for this book! Everywhere I go I meet Christians—many of them leaders—on the verge of burning out, caving in, and laying down their dreams. My friend Mark Jobe hasn't just written this book: he has wept it, lived it, and prayed it into being over many years pastoring one of the most exciting and transformational churches in America. I have no doubt that his message will bring hope to those who feel stuck, and that it will help others to articulate their unspoken weariness and boredom. I commend *Unstuck* particularly to pastors seeking to lead others through life's many stages.

—Pete Greig
Founding champion of 24-7 Prayer, Director of Prayer for Alpha International, author of *God on Mute*

Unstuck strikes right at the heart of an uncomfortable place where many of us have found ourselves. More importantly, it shows us the way out—God's way. During a ministry of almost thirty years, God has used Mark Jobe to get thousands of people unstuck from the situations in which they found themselves and get them into a life full of release, significance, and joy. Using the biblical experience of Elijah, Mark Jobe integrates the stories of how God gets real people today out of the doldrums and back into a dynamic, fresh walk with the Lord. You'll love this book and be ready to live a new chapter of your own life!

—Dr. Mike Pocock
Senior Professor and Chairman Emeritus at Dallas Theological Seminary

There are many people who feel that God is angry or upset with them because of personal challenges they've been forced to go through unfairly or without a warning. In this impactful and insightful glimpse into the life of Elijah, Mark Jobe shares with us a fresh and new perspective on how God designs such situations for our growth.

This book is a must for every Christian leader, because if you haven't already, you will eventually experience a cave experience. *Unstuck* is your answer for overcoming it.

—James T. Meeks
Senior Pastor of Salem Baptist Church of Chicago, retired Illinois State Senator

Unstuck is a true to life snapshot of doing church in a big city like Chicago. Pastors and leaders face the challenge of meeting overwhelming need with limited resources. We are burdened by the brokenness of urban life: violence, poverty, drug abuse, homelessness, and lack of education. However, Jobe clearly reveals how any ministry is most hindered, not by these issues, but by our own finite thinking. As we submit to God's kingdom mindset, we will see the Church—both locally and globally—get unstuck.

—Rev. Wilfredo "Choco" DeJesus
Senior Pastor of New Life Covenant

To my wife, Dee.
She was a fan of this book before I ever wrote it.

CONTENTS

INTRODUCTION

No one wants to be stuck. I personally hate the feeling of being trapped in traffic, stalled in long lines at the airport, blocked in a parking space, or stranded in a Chicago snowstorm. Maybe you are like me and start thinking that the stoplight isn't working because it takes so long before turning green. We have clinical words to describe the anxiety and stress that being stuck produces. "Cleithrophobia" (great spelling bee material) is the phobia of being trapped, locked in, unable to leave, the fear of being stuck. In spite of our strong aversion to being trapped, countless people—maybe you're one of them—find themselves living unhappily in this most detestable of conditions, stuck in life.

Nicholas White, a thirty-four-year-old production manager, was returning from a break on a Friday evening when the elevator in his New York City office building became stuck between floors. He had no watch, no cellphone, no water, and no food—only a pack of Rolaids.

He paced, called for help, banged on the elevator walls, and even tried to climb out through the ceiling. He finally managed to pry open the elevator doors, only to be faced with a brick wall.

Nearly two days later, he reached his breaking point. White, not a religious man, prayed for help. At four o'clock

Sunday afternoon, almost delirious from thirst and by now resigned to his fate, he heard a voice on the intercom asking if anyone was there. Finally he was rescued by the paramedics. He had been stuck for forty-one hours.

White had no lasting physical side effects from his elevator experience, but by his own admission it left him emotionally troubled. He never discovered why the elevator stopped. In the weeks following his ordeal White lost his job of fifteen years, lost all contact with former coworkers, lost his apartment, and spent all his savings. He later acknowledged, "It wasn't so much the elevator that changed me as my reaction to it."[1]

What a powerful insight. It is not getting stuck that changes us as much as how we respond to getting stuck that transforms us.

This book is for anyone who really (I mean *really*) wants to get unstuck. The insights, stories, and principles developed in these chapters are aimed at helping you discover what is keeping you from moving forward and inspiring you to break out into your new season of life.

The issues that get *us* stuck, and keep us there, are often difficult to identify.

Like carbon monoxide, they are hard to detect but deadly if we don't deal with them. Nicholas White did not know why his elevator stopped moving, and neither did Troy Fredrickson know at first why he was lying on the floor of his house, barely able to crawl to the door. A few years ago, Fredrickson, chief of a small fire department, and his wife were awakened by their young daughter who was complaining of feeling sick and vomiting. Fredrickson had a slight headache himself. But he helped wash his daughter and prepared a clean bed for her. A short time later, his slight headache became a splitting headache, worse than any migraine he had ever suffered. Fredrickson was climbing the stairs to get some medication when his firefighter training kicked in. He realized what was wrong. He and his daughter were suffering from carbon monoxide poisoning, the result of a malfunctioning furnace. He immediately rushed toward the front door but Fredrickson passed out before he could reach it. When he came to, he was barely able to crawl to the door and open it. Once outside, he fought to stay conscious until help arrived. "If I had not had the training I have," Fredrickson later reflected, "we could have written it off as the flu and gone back to bed. We would have slept to death."[2]

Those words—"We would have slept to death"—could be said of anyone stuck too long in life. If you stay too long in the poisonous environment of being stuck, you too will sleep to death. You may have lived ensnared so long that you feel your life's energy being drained as you struggle to crawl toward an exit door. Maybe you feel as though you are gasping for a breath of spiritual fresh air. Chances are you have wrestled with the challenge of being stuck, so you know the feeling and have tasted the frustration.

Getting unstuck does not mean you need to move to another state, change your marital status, find a new job, switch churches, replace a business partner, alter your hair color, shift your major in college, or get a new tattoo. It does mean making new choices in the middle of your current circumstances. For most of us it means a fresh encounter with God that exposes our issues and awakens us to the new seasons to which He is calling us. These chapters will help you begin the process of getting permanently unstuck.

This book is based on the story of a man, a cave, and his God.

The story of Elijah and his cave has been recounted for almost three thousand years. The renowned prophet is an important figure in Judaism, Islam, and Christianity. Thousands of people each year visit Elijah's Cave in Haifa, Israel (not to be confused with the cave in this book). In Jewish homes all over the world each week the name of Elijah is invoked in a ritual that marks the end of the Sabbath (Shabbat). Elijah is considered one of the greatest prophets to ever walk the earth. His journey into the infamous cave and his extraordinary passage out is one of the most compelling stories in history.

Elijah's cave experience became a key turning point that redefined his future. Anyone struggling with the frustration of being stuck in life will gain inspiration and useful insight from Elijah's journey. This is a simple yet profound story of a man who overcomes his cave.

Over the past twenty-five years, I have had the incredible opportunity of working with literally thousands of people from all walks of life in the great city of Chicago. I have been astounded by the number of people who are seriously stuck, letting life pass them by and frustrated about what to do. They are not trapped in a physical sense, like Nicholas White in his nightmare elevator or Troy Fredrickson in his poison-filled home. They are stuck in a much more severe way—not between floors, but between this moment and the next. Many have lived so long in this suffocating, stale environment that they cannot remember what it feels like to breathe the air outside. As you read this book I hope you can begin to fill your lungs with the fresh air of a new season and take the first step out of your cave.

CHAPTER 1

HELP, I'M STUCK!

I was only twenty-one but already I felt stuck. I lay there on my grandmother's floral-patterned couch as waves of discouragement washed over me. Every bone in my body seemed to ache. I had tried as hard as I knew how, but was tired of spinning my wheels and going nowhere. I wasn't sure I had the energy or even the desire to continue on. There I was, only five months into my ministry, and I was already physically depleted, emotionally discouraged, and spiritually dry. I had to admit it, I was stuck.

My mind raced back.

My second week in Chicago I was awakened at two o'clock in the morning by loud banging noises outside my window. When I peered out I saw a dozen or more young men running down the middle of the street shouting with guns in hand. Another shot rang out. I remember ducking and thinking, *What have I gotten myself into?* It was hard going back to sleep with the adrenaline still pumping. A week later my fiancée (now wife) Dee was waiting for me in her car. As I walked toward her I could tell something was wrong. Just minutes earlier a pregnant sixteen-year-old girl was stabbed in the stomach in a gang-related incident right in front of Dee. When I opened the car door she was teary eyed and shaking uncontrollably. The puddle of blood on the sidewalk was a grim reminder of the senseless violence that plagued the neighborhood around our church.

The congregation was small, young, and chaotic—-to say the least. Our Sunday services were unpredictable, as well. Like the Sunday we had a blind guest speaker and Charlie, the 275-pound neighbor, showed up to our evening worship service a little drunk. That day our ushers must have been distracted, because Charlie made it from the doorway entrance all the way up the aisle and face-to-face with our unsuspecting—and blind—guest speaker. Charlie tried to confiscate the microphone from him, but our ex-convict ushers caught on and quickly subdued Charlie. They promptly escorted him out of the building. Charlie shouted slurred obscenities all the way back down the center aisle and out the door.

GUNS AND GANGBANGERS

One Sunday morning after the service I noticed that people had bottlenecked at our exit doors. Someone came running up to me and said, "Hey, Pastor, we got a situation." "A situation" around our church was always code for crisis. A man was waving a gun on the street in front of the church entrance. By the time I made it outside, the man had the gun pointed at the head of another terrified man, whom he had pushed up against a parked car. Without thinking I rushed to intervene. I found myself standing in front of an angry gunman with my little congregation huddled in the entrance of our church building in disbelief at their impulsive young pastor. At that moment the thought crossed my mind that I could have called the police and let them handle it. It was too late for that.

I felt a little like Peter after he jumped out of the boat to walk on the water and realized he needed a life jacket. I mustered up the most pastoral tone my twenty-one-year-old vocal cords could manage and said, "Hey you. I'm the pastor of this church. You're scaring my people. So put down your gun and let that guy go."

He looked up at me a little startled. I wasn't sure if he was about to turn the gun on me or follow my instructions. I could tell he wasn't sure if he believed me, but after glancing up at the heads poking out of the church entrance he slowly put down his revolver. He tried to convince me that he was on my side, that we were "community partners" and he was just performing a type of community service, getting rid of scum like the guy he was still holding down. I assured him that there were better ways of cleaning up the neighborhood and persuaded him to put away his revolver so our people could get to their cars.

To say that we were attracting "unchurched" people was a bit of an understatement.

One young man who started showing up at our services was a gangbanger from the neighborhood who, because he had been shot in the head, was partially paralyzed. He walked with difficulty and he talked with a slight slur, but his gangbanging attitude was healthy and intact. We started getting complaints from young women in the church that he was sitting

TO SAY THAT we were attracting "unchurched" people was a bit of an understatement.

next to them and whispering obscene comments to them during the service. I approached him one morning to let him know that he was welcome to worship with us, but the next time he started talking dirty to one of our sisters he would be out the door. I alerted our ex-convict ushers to keep an eye on him.

Sure enough, a couple of weeks later, in the middle of our worship time, I saw him lean over toward a young woman, a Bible-college student. Her face turned red and her jaw dropped. From the front I motioned to our two ushers to deal with him. One of them, a big ex-drug dealer named Jose, made his way down the aisle, leaned over, and had a talk with the young man. The conversation was tense. Our gangbanger friend wrapped his legs around his chair and grabbed on to his seat with a look of defiance. The next thing I saw was two big ushers carrying our dirty-talking gangbanger and his chair down the long aisle toward the exit doors. They plopped him on the church stairway outside our main entrance. After that, there was a new respect for our no-nonsense usher team.

With nonstop crises at my door, little sleep, poor eating habits, and a full schedule, I started to wear down. The needs of the community began to overwhelm me. Our resources were scarce. Demands were increasing and my once bright vision was quickly fading. I believed God had led me here. But now I was wearing down. I was starting to feel like God had left me to fend for myself.

BURNED OUT IN FOUR MONTHS

Only a few months earlier I had walked slowly up the concrete stairs of the former Russian Orthodox church. It was my first day on the job and there was nobody else in the building. I strolled down the middle aisle to the small, makeshift office behind the stage and sat on an old wooden chair. My thoughts were interrupted by the scurrying of squirrel feet on the old tin ceiling. Apparently they liked my preaching and decided to make this their home church.

This small church on the southwest side of Chicago had about eighteen people and could afford to pay me only a minimal part-time salary. They had been looking for a pastor for about two years but were having a difficult time finding anyone willing to accept the salary and live in the neighborhood. In fact, at least one seminary candidate had driven by the building and rolled down his window but refused to get out of his car. Instead he locked his doors and sped away. Sunday morning we had a piano player to lead the singing, but Sunday night and Wednesdays the group sang a cappella out of hymnbooks. The small leadership committee was so desperate they asked me, a single twenty-one-year-old fresh out of college and with no pastoral experience, to be their pastor. I was naïve enough to say yes. Desperate and naïve—we made a great combination.

A businessman from the congregation felt sorry for me, so he allowed me to stay rent free in a building he owned that was used for offices and warehouse space. I lived in one room and shared the bathroom with the office workers. I had a mattress on the floor and a flimsy table with two yellow vinyl-covered chairs. My books were stacked on the floor and I had mouse-traps strategically placed around my mattress to ward off the little critters that made their rounds at night.

The low pay and Spartan living conditions were not the greatest challenge. There were people in need everywhere I turned. I was single, young, full of unrestrained idealism, and wanting to help people. I soon found myself in a whirl-wind of activity. I decided I would personally try to visit as many homes as possible in the community. It was the dead of winter, so not many people were hanging out on Chicago's frigid streets. I recruited any willing partner I could and we started visiting homes. On top of visiting people four nights a week, I was teaching three times a week, mentoring new people, teaching guitar lessons, hosting leadership meetings, counseling people in crisis, trying to raise money, organiz-ing work crews, and preparing for my upcoming wedding. I even took on the task of emptying the bell tower of decades of pigeon droppings that filled twenty garbage bags. I don't seem to remember any class called "Bell Tower Cleaning 101" in seminary.

Several had left the mission church since I arrived. They opposed the changes I was making. Apparently our clapping and my guitar playing during the service were unacceptable to the old guard. So I managed to take a group of twenty down to fifteen in a few short weeks. We had no worship team or functioning Sunday school, and our offerings were pretty pa-thetic. Our building, constructed in 1910, was falling apart. Gang members hung out on the front steps of the church like they owned the street corner. I was supposed to be getting married in a couple of months and I could barely afford to live on my $8,000-a-year salary myself, let alone support a wife. I had no car of my own, no savings, and no insurance. I had been running hard from early in the morning to late at night with very few visible results to show. *Maybe*, I thought, *I'm not cut out to be a pastor.*

Since I had no insurance, my grandmother's doctor agreed to see me free of charge in the neighboring state of Indiana. I wasn't sure what was wrong but I knew I was out of energy and feeling very sick. After examining me the doctor sternly warned me that I needed bed rest and that my health was at risk if I did not take care of myself. That week on my grandmother's couch, I spent a full day moaning and complaining. I was semi-delirious, battling bouts of fever and drifting in and out of sleep.

"Why have You let this happen, God?" was my faint prayer. "How did I end up here, anyway?" I remembered what my last pastor told me when I talked to him about the possibility of working with a church in the inner city of Chicago. He looked at me somberly and said, "The city chews up and spits out pastors left and right. You'd better be sure God has called you there." At that moment, as I was lying on the couch, those words echoed in my mind. Uncertainty was settling in. I definitely felt chewed up and spit out. Maybe I *had* made a mistake. Maybe I shouldn't be there.

Eventually I summoned the strength to wrap myself in a blanket and made my way to the basement. I paced the length of that basement floor and continued grumbling to God that

I had done all that He had asked me to and that He had led me to a dead-end situation. I felt stuck and abandoned. The more I complained, the worse I felt. A dark cloud of bleakness settled over my prayers of complaint. In frustration I told God that I did not want to do this anymore. God was silent.

OUT OF THE BASEMENT

The next day I was too exhausted to keep complaining and too worn out to keep moaning. I just lay there wrapped in my blanket silent before God. Finally, in the silence of that dark basement, the still small whisper of God's voice began to pierce through the confusing noise of my spiritual dissonance. I slowly began to realize I had become too busy with my mission to make time to listen to God. The voice of people's needs and my drive to succeed had made me slip away from the most important call, my own walk with God.

Over the next couple of days I did some deep soul searching. I began to see some of the unhealthy pressures that were driving me. An older, well-established pastor I knew let people know that he doubted I would succeed at leading a church in the city. I started to think that I had to work hard to prove that I wouldn't fail. My identity was wrapped up in whether I failed or succeeded. To further complicate matters, I was dealing with unfinished business. I had been hurt by a group of people I expected to be supportive but who instead had been critical. In my mind they walked away when I needed them most. In addition I came face-to-face with an ugly arrogance in my soul. I had fallen into the trap of thinking that it was my job to fix people, save people, and meet people's needs.

I caught myself praying, "Forgive me for attempting to do in my own strength what only You can do in the power of Your Spirit." I came to realize that God didn't need a miniature, pseudo-messiah frantically trying to do the work of the real Messiah. I admitted my self-reliance and lack of God dependence. I felt broken over the arrogance that had led me to such a dark place but humbled by the amazing grace of a God who was drawing me out. This was a turning point, a defining moment. When I finally walked up those basement stairs, I knew I had heard the whisper of God's Spirit.

I decided I could not do ministry the same way anymore. As I drove back to Chicago, I knew change was coming. I was driving back to the same pressure, people problems, and financial crises, but I felt different. I had a new awareness of my own weakness, a consciousness of my dependence on God.

In the months that followed, the little church began to experience unexpected breakthroughs. Suddenly people who had been resistant were now responding. It appeared as though an invisible lid was taken off our struggling congregation. Our worship services were brimming with a new sense of God's presence. What I had failed to do in my self-effort was happening as I stepped aside and made room for God. People from many backgrounds and diverse neighborhoods in Chicago began making their way to the old brick building on 44th and Paulina. This was the beginning of a new season.

SHAPED BY THE STRUGGLE

That brief but defining basement experience helped shape me in profound ways. My personal meltdown impressed upon me the importance of not going ahead of God, nor lagging behind Him but seeking to stay in step with what He is doing. I have often remembered the painful experience of being too busy for God and the frustration of trying to pursue my mission in my own strength. The early lessons I learned in the struggle to exit my cave have profoundly shaped my approach to life.

We all have our own sticking points that keep us from moving forward. I don't know your story, but I do know that a new season is within your grasp. I hope you are beginning to hear the spiritual whisper calling you toward the exit. That divine undertone, stirring a holy discontent that makes you long to live differently. I pray you find your heart even now being awakened to the possibilities of stepping bravely into your new season.

CHAPTER 2

WE ALL GET STUCK SOMETIME

Junior was struggling with a major addiction when we talked.

We sat together in a cheap, greasy diner. His eyes were red and his face was unshaven. He looked as if he had slept in the garage the night before. "I'm stuck," he said like a man that had lost hope. "I know the kind of father, husband, and man I want to be, but I keep falling into the same trap of addiction over and over. I'm not sure that I will ever be able to change. My wife is sick of me, my kids avoid me, and my relatives don't want to deal with it anymore. I'm tired of making promises I don't keep, starting things I don't finish, and being trapped in this ongoing cycle of repeated failure. I don't know what to do anymore."

Angie confided that her life was stuck, as well.

She fidgeted with her hands as she spoke, her eyes carefully avoiding mine. "This is very uncomfortable to talk about," she said with a tremble in her voice. "Excuse me—I'm kind of nervous. I'm just going to say it. I was sexually molested from the age of nine until I was twelve, and I was raped when I was twenty years old." As she continued, she became agitated. "I hate the man who did this to me when I was just a child." She went on to describe how she loathed the sight of her own face in the mirror. Her shame and insecurities had led her through a series of brief and unfulfilled relationships with men. "I don't want to live this way any longer. I have been repeating the same mistakes over and over. I am ready to change, but I'm not sure I know how. I feel stuck."

Wayne blurted out what he was feeling.

"I'm stuck and frustrated!" There was exasperation in the voice on the other end of the phone line. "I know I have gifts and a call on my life, but here I am!" Wayne had started down the ministry road right out of college and had shown a lot of promise. Then he took a break from full-time ministry to work in the business world. As a sales account executive he was doing great professionally, but he was frustrated personally. He bought the suburban dream home and the kid-friendly minivan. He was sending his children to good schools. But he was obviously unhappy. "I'm climbing the corporate ladder. My bosses like me. I'm good at what I do, but something is not right," he said, aggravated. "I have tasted success, but I know I am called to make a greater difference with my life. I need help to get unstuck."

I had a similar conversation with a young married woman.

Susan stepped into my office and I could tell by the look on her face she was in pain. Just two years earlier she was the picture of happiness. She had married the man of her dreams. They were starting a new life together, excited about their future and ready to make a difference. Now she sat in my office with her husband at her side. Her shoulders were slumped and the spark was missing from her eyes. She stared blankly and confided: "I'm stuck. I feel like a bruised and battered, broken wife." Her marriage had not gone as smoothly as she had hoped. She had lost trust in her husband. Her view of their future was once gleaming bright, but now it was dark and unclear. "I'm afraid I made a mistake. I feel like I will spend the rest of my life regretting my decision. I'm afraid I will be stuck in a cycle of unhappiness for the rest of my life. I don't know what to do. I need help."

James was a pastor and felt just as trapped.

"I am not sure what happened to me," James said, shaking his head. "I remember when I was full of faith and excited about the ministry God called me to." He took a sip of his coffee and then blurted out, "How can I pastor a church when I am spiritually dry?" He lowered his voice and added, "I never knew it would be so hard to lead people. All the criticism, pressure, expectations, and people problems has done something to my soul. I'm not sure I want to continue on. If I could quit and get another job today, I think I would. But I feel stuck. I have to be a spiritual leader when I feel spiritually lifeless. I'm not sure what to do."

"I FEEL LIKE A bruised and battered, broken wife."

You may relate to Junior or Angie, Wayne or Susan or even James. They are just a few of the hundreds of people from all walks of life who finally made the same admission: "I'm stuck and I don't know how to move forward."

A SPINELESS KING, A GUTSY PROPHET, AND A TRAMPY QUEEN

One of the greatest spiritual leaders in history felt the very same way as the people in these stories you just read about. He had an astonishing track record, yet he spiraled down to the dark hole of discouragement. His physical exhaustion and emotional disappointment ultimately slipped into spiritual letdown. In his blackest hour he ended up in a cave. Elijah's cave experience, however, turned out to be the most transformative episode of his life. Elijah the prophet from Tishbe (pronounced Tish-bee) lived in the ninth century BC during an especially dark and turbulent time in Israel. King Ahab was the most egocentric and spineless king to sit on the throne of Israel (1 Kings 21:25–26). He married a woman named Jezebel, the infamous daughter of the king of Sidon. Her reputation as manipulative and power-hungry has made her the archetype of the wicked woman in American literature. Look up the name Jezebel in the dictionary and you will see words like "impudent," "shameless," "morally unrestrained," "gold-digger," "floozy," "tramp," or "wench" associated with this name. Needless to say, Jezebel does not make the list of most popular names given to cute little newborn girls. Seriously, how many girls named Jezebel do you know? Ahab and Jezebel's marriage hurled the northern kingdom into a dark season dominated by worship of Jezebel's personal favorite god, Baal.

As this was happening, Elijah made the gutsy move of confronting Ahab and pronouncing an epic drought on the land that ended up lasting more than three full years. To ensure that Elijah had water to drink while the rest of Israel dried up, God instructed him to lie low by a brook named Cherith. Streams shrank, crops withered, cattle died, and as the famine intensified so did Ahab's hatred for Elijah, the man he blamed for the national economic crisis caused by the drought. Ahab declared Elijah the number one enemy of the state and launched a national manhunt for the elusive prophet. Meanwhile, Elijah survived by drinking the water from the brook and eating the food delivered to him by ravens.

In time, even the brook at Cherith dried up and God moved Elijah to the town of Zarephath (you will not be required to remember this name), where he stayed with a poor widow and her son. God continued to provide miraculously for their survival while the prophet lived with this impoverished family.

THE SHOWDOWN MOMENT

Finally, God told Elijah the time had come to present himself to the now furious and exasperated King Ahab. So, after three years in hiding, Elijah challenged Ahab to gather the people and his 450 pagan prophets on Mount Carmel for a showdown. Everyone turned out for the big event. There on the summit of the mountain, Elijah sternly rebuked the people of Israel for wavering in their allegiance between God and Baal. They remained silent. He proposed a contest to determine once and for all who Israel would follow. This was the test: the pagan prophets built an altar for Baal and Elijah built an altar for God. Then the prophets slaughtered two bulls, one for each altar, and laid the offering on top of the wood. But instead of lighting the wood, the prophets were challenged to pray for supernatural fire to devour the offering. The people of Israel agreed they would serve the one who proved he was most powerful by sending fire from heaven.

The prophets of Baal went first. With fanatic enthusiasm, 450 prophets danced, shouted, and cut themselves in a bloody and frenzied attempt to call fire down from heaven. From morning until evening the pagan prophets continued their frantic rituals until, exhausted, they relinquished their turn to Elijah.

With the confidence of a man on a mission, Elijah calmly gathered the people and requested that the altar of sacrifice be drenched three times with water. He then stepped forward and prayed a simple prayer: "Lord, the God of Abraham, Isaac and Israel, let it be known today that you are God in Israel and that I am your servant and have done all these things at your command. Answer me, Lord, answer me, so these people will know that you, Lord, are God, and that you are turning their hearts back again" (1 Kings 18:36–37).

Suddenly fire fell from the sky and with intense heat consumed the bulls, the wood, the stones, and the earth around the altar. The awestruck crowd fell to their faces and began to chant, "The Lord—He is God! The Lord—He is God!" Imagine how Elijah must have felt. The altar is smoldering in the background. Tens of thousands of people have fallen to the ground and continue to chant, "The Lord—He is God!" The 450 exhausted and bleeding prophets of Baal are in shock and disbelief. King Ahab is looking at Elijah with a face that says, "Who are you?" A new sense of fear and respect for this bearded prophet that calls fire from heaven overwhelms him. The entire nation now knows Elijah and his God have been vindicated.

BUT I THOUGHT THIS WAS OVER!

It appeared that Elijah had accomplished his purpose, won the battle, and could ultimately put this three-year ordeal behind him. He could finally stop hiding, go back to his home, put on his favorite slippers, and return to life as usual. He breathed a sigh of relief and prepared his victory speech. There was one final detail to which he must attend. Queen Jezebel had refused to be present for the contest of the prophets, opting instead to stay at her summer palace in Jezreel. Elijah's final duty was to inform Jezebel that her prophets had lost and that he had won the divine contest.

Elijah told Ahab, "Go, eat and drink, for there is the sound of a heavy rain" (1 Kings 18:41). Now that the people of Israel had turned back to God it was time for the drought to end. Elijah advised Ahab to prepare his chariot and speed back to his home in Jezreel before the downpour. As the sky grew dark with ominous rain clouds, the power of the Lord came upon Elijah and he ran the twenty miles to Jezreel faster than Ahab's chariot. Apparently Roger Bannister was not the first to run a four-minute mile. Elijah was unstoppable and at the top of his game.

Clearly Elijah anticipated that Jezebel would fall to her face in utter defeat and admit that he and his God had won the contest fairly. He couldn't wait to hear Jezebel give her concession speech. Scripture doesn't tell us how Ahab told his domineering wife that her prophets had failed and had all been executed. I can only imagine her shock and disbelief. I can see her eyes slanting and her lips tightening as the veins begin to pop out on her forehead. I can hear her hiss, *"Elijah,"* and then whisper in a murderous tone, "I want him dead by tomorrow. Tell him I will have his head if it is the last thing I do!"

Elijah must have paced excitedly outside the palace gates waiting to hear good news. Instead, a messenger came out to meet Elijah with a grim message from the queen. Robert Deffinbaugh pictures the moment this way: "Elijah hears footsteps approaching the door and watches intently as it swings open. Neither Ahab nor Jezebel emerge, but one of the servants, who conveys a message from Jezebel to the prophet: He has twenty-four hours to live. Jezebel is going to kill him, just like he killed the 450 prophets of Baal."[1]

Elijah was in shock. This was not what he expected. He must have slowly walked away, stunned by the words of the messenger and trying to process what had just occurred.

WHEN SOMETHING CRACKS INSIDE

It happened suddenly. It was as if something cracked inside his soul. This spiritual superhero began to melt. Jezebel's threat gripped Elijah to his very core. The exhilaration of yesterday's victory came crashing down around him. Unshakable faith gave way to uncontrollable fear. Stunned and reeling from Jezebel's message, Elijah turned and ran for his life. Only minutes before he had run with high-spirited energy at the speed of chariots toward the promise of a brighter future. Now he ran in the opposite direction driven by overwhelming fear. His panic-stricken run took him a hundred miles away to the town of Beersheba, known as the "gateway to the desert."

It was as if something cracked inside his soul.

In Beersheba he stopped only long enough to drop off his assistant; then he headed straight for the most remote desert. For upwards of eight more hours he stumbled through the dry, rocky countryside. The farther he traveled the more isolated the countryside became. He spotted a broom tree—a shrub with a broad canopy of leaves—and plopped down under its branches. Then he hoarsely whispered a desperate prayer through his heavy breathing: "'I have had enough, Lord,' he said. 'Take my life; I am no better than my ancestors'" (1 Kings 19:4).

Exhaustion and disappointment withered into discouragement in the hot desert sun. His eyes closed and Elijah fell into a deep sleep. Sometime later he suddenly awakened to find by his head a meal prepared and waiting for him. He ate in silence and fell asleep again. After a long nap he was awakened a second time and was told to eat and drink to prepare for a long journey.

Elijah then traveled forty days and about two hundred miles through the Wilderness of Paran, until he reached the iconic mountain of God at the southern tip of Sinai, Mount Horeb. Nearly six hundred years earlier God had appeared to

Moses at this same place. Some still referred to this mountain as "the mountain of God." All told, some sixty-three chapters of the Old Testament are devoted to events that took place at this mountain.[2] This was not just any mountain. This was the mountain of God. Elijah climbed the rocky mountainside until he spotted a cave. He peered inside this shadowy cavern, then groped his way to a dark corner where he spent the night.

This cave would prove to be the setting for one of the most dramatic encounters recorded in all of Scripture. Here Elijah would confront his deepest issues and face the forces that had driven him into darkness. Here he would have a life-altering encounter. This is the story of a man, a cave, and his God.

CHAPTER 3

THE SEVEN STICKING POINTS

A couple of years ago I decided at the last minute to take a trip from Chicago to Atlanta. It was my son Josiah's birthday, and he was excited to see Christian rapper Lecrae perform at the Georgia Dome. So my son, daughter, a friend their age, and I piled in my car and started off on our road trip. We were laughing, telling stories, and listening to music. It was just like any road trip with three rowdy teenagers.

A few miles outside of Indianapolis the SUV driving next to us hit a patch of black ice and literally rammed us off the road. It's scary to be forced onto the median of an expressway at sixty-five miles an hour. This median happened to be populated by bushes and small trees, so we went flying through the shrubbery. I felt like we were in one of those movies where a car goes hurtling through the jungle and all the audience sees are branches slapping the windshield. The difference was I was *in* this movie and not eating popcorn in a theater.

I braced myself for impact but, to my amazement and relief, we came to a full stop after hitting a row of small trees.

My three teenage passengers were shaken up but uninjured. The driver of the SUV that forced us off the road was stopped nearby. Half dazed, I walked over to speak with the apologetic driver, who was wearing her pajamas and hair curlers. As I was walking back to my car, something unexpected happened. My son shouted a warning, tires squealed, and I jumped into my car just in time. An out-of-control vehicle careened off the road right past us. Over the next couple of minutes we watched as about twenty cars and one semitruck collided in a major expressway pileup. The entire road was strewn with the wreckage. My car and many others were totaled. I-65 was closed. We were all stuck.

A few days later, the insurance company called to ask me how this twenty-car pileup started. The agent wanted to know the sequence of events that led to dozens of ruined vehicles, injured people, and a clogged expressway. As I began to tell the story, I realized there were a lot of "ifs" in my account. If the lady in curlers had only stayed in her lane. If I had just driven a little slower. If the salt trucks had started earlier. If the car behind us had paid better attention. If the semitruck driver had pulled to the side of the road instead of slamming on the brakes. A series of mistakes compounded the problem that led to hundreds of travelers being stuck and dozens of people being taken to the hospital.

As you look back over your own story and try to explain how you ended up stuck, you may discover the same thing I did. There are many "ifs" that have affected your journey. Typically it is not one event that ends up getting you stuck; it's a series of events—and your response to those events—that leads you to your current predicament.

I have seen many vibrant, gifted people unexpectedly end up stalled on the side of the road. They are scratching their heads and wondering what in the world

THERE ARE MANY "ifs" that have affected your journey.

happened to them. Often they linger so long in that spiritual traffic jam that their soul drains, their dreams evaporate, and they dismiss their vision as a season of naïve, youthful idealism.

Common to almost every person's journey to "stuck" are at least a few of these seven sticking points. These sticking points appear in Elijah's story too. He had to confront each of them in order to step out of his cave. These seven sticking points are traps that send millions into frustrating dead-end living. Not every person gets stuck on all seven points but most of us struggle with some combination of them.

STICKING POINT ONE:
ISOLATED LIVING

The first sticking point is isolated living. Solitude is a great spiritual discipline, but isolation is an emotionally lethal condition that most of us struggle with. Isolation is unhealthy in virtually any season and context of life. The most dangerous place in the world is to be alone with our dark thinking and unresolved issues.

Like many of us Elijah's instinct was to run from his problem and isolate himself from the people he needed most at a critical time in his journey. Through the cave experience

Elijah was called to break his cycle of isolation. This maverick prophet would have to relearn the power of relationship in his new season of life. Stepping out and staying out of the cave requires cultivating healthy community that safeguards us from returning to the same cave.

STICKING POINT TWO: DISTORTED THINKING

The second sticking point is distorted thinking. Distorted thinking is like a bad recording that plays over and over in our heads convincing us of a false reality. Eventually that distorted message shapes and defines the way we see our world. Those messages in our head repeat lies about our identity and destiny. Distorted thinking inevitably drives us to missteps that only perpetuate our state of being stuck. Like insects trapped in the sticky web of a hungry spider, the more we struggle to escape the more entangled we become.

God had to interrupt Elijah's mental recording by challenging his thinking. If our thoughts are not being shaped by truth, then they will soon be shaped by whatever message rings loudest and is repeated most in our head. This message will determine our reflex response to life.

STICKING POINT THREE: IMPAIRED HEARING

The third sticking point is impaired hearing. Many of us have so much "white noise" in our life we struggle to hear the clear voice of God. Webster's dictionary defines white noise as a constant background noise, one that drowns out other sounds. It is virtually impossible to hear the gentle whisper of God while engaged in fear-filled, anxious, insecure self-pitying conversations that rumble loudly in our heads.

Recently after I spoke at an event, I lingered for some time talking, hearing stories, and praying for many people. Eventually the organizers needed to close down the auditorium, so they ushered me out of the hall and briskly walked me to my car. Behind me I heard someone calling my name. I turned around to see a man in his thirties running to catch up with me.

"I know you have to go," he said, "but I desperately need you to pray for me. I have been a believer for several years, but I have never heard the voice of God speak to me." He went on to say that he had called out and sought after God but was met with heavenly silence. "Could you pray that God would speak to me?" he asked.

I read the earnestness in his face and said, "No."

He was taken aback. Why on earth would a pastor refuse to pray that God would speak to him? "If you truly are a son of God, I don't need to ask that God would speak to you," I replied. "I need to pray that your ears will open up to hear God when He does speak to you." I explained that I have three children that I deeply love and I cannot imagine not speaking to them. But there have been plenty of times when I have spoken to one of my kids and they have not been able to hear me because their music or the television drowned out my voice.

So that evening, on that busy sidewalk, instead of praying that God would speak to this man, I put my hands on his shoulders and prayed that he would silence the white noise that was hindering him from hearing the voice of his Creator.

Many sincere people of faith are frustrated by their inability to hear from God clearly. The voices of their own thoughts, fears, anxieties, insecurities, and misperceptions often ring so loud that the voice of God is often imperceptible.

STICKING POINT FOUR:
WARPED IDENTITY

The fourth sticking point that keeps us from moving forward is a warped identity. The mental picture we carry of ourselves defines how we interact with our world. The battle for personal identity rages from kindergarten playgrounds to the offices in corporate America. How you see yourself and who you think you are will affect your life as deeply as any thought you have.

MANY SINCERE people of faith are frustrated by their inability to hear from God clearly.

I had the opportunity to speak to several hundred youth in Quito, Ecuador. I heard that the center of the earth, the line dividing the northern hemisphere from the southern hemisphere, was just a few miles outside of the city of Quito. So we took a trip to see it. Sure enough there was an enormous monument built in that spot called *La Mitad Del Mundo* or The Middle of the World. A yellow line marking the equator was drawn for several hundred feet. It went down the center of the buildings and was painted in bright yellow right through the middle aisle of a small chapel. People took pictures with one foot north of the line and one foot south of the line, standing on two hemispheres at once.

Our guide told us that you can spin an egg on the head of a nail and it won't fall off if you are in the center of the equator. When I asked him if we could try it he said we could but we would have to walk about 800 feet north to the real equator line. I looked at him puzzled. He explained that in 1936 when scientists determined the equator line, their instruments were not as accurate as current GPS systems. Their calculations were off by about 800 feet. Every year over 500,000 tourists visit the Middle of the Earth and take pictures on the famous yellow line. Most are unaware that the real middle of the earth, the Equator, has no visible yellow line or monument and is actually several hundred feet away.

Elijah believed that he was alone, abandoned by God, and a failure. He was 800 feet from the truth. The mental picture drawn in our mind, like the misleading yellow line, often does not reflect reality. Instead, it reflects the distortions that we have believed. We can only see the real picture when we look at ourselves from a divine perspective. God's GPS is always right.

STICKING POINT FIVE: NEGLECTED ISSUES

The fifth sticking point is neglected issues or unfinished business. These are issues that we have avoided in the past, and they become one of the greatest causes of living stuck. We all tend to avoid painful issues. Unfortunately, avoiding our issues postpones the immediate pain but actually increases our long-term problems exponentially.

She sat uncomfortably in my office. "I wanted to meet with you to share my story," she said timidly. She explained that she had visited our church about two years before. She had never been to a Christian church before so, although she was drawn to the joy she saw in people, she was frightened by what it would mean to come back. Over the next two years her life spiraled into deeper anxiety and a paralyzing depression. Her sister was extremely concerned about her and encouraged her to look for God. She decided to give New Life Church another try.

"That morning you spoke about the need to forgive and release people that have hurt us in order to move forward," she said. "I cried during the entire message. I knew for the first time in my life that God was speaking to me." She painfully revealed how she had been molested by a relative at an early age and raped by a man she trusted when she was older. The shame, anger, and resentment swirled together into the overwhelming darkness of depression. "I decided to go to the woman's encounter retreat," she continued. "For the first time in my life I stepped out of denial and confronted my pain. With the help of some sisters, I was able to admit what had happened, embrace God's forgiveness, and start the journey toward forgiving," she explained. "I had been avoiding my painful past, but now for the first time in my life I actually feel hope." When she finally looked up at me, she added, "I wish I had done this a long time ago."

I have heard this story repeated over and over. The more we run from our issues, the more they control our destiny and affect every area of our life. When we turn around and face them, when we go to the hard places, only then can we finally move forward.

STICKING POINT SIX: BLURRED CALLING

Sticking point number six is a blurred calling. Coming to terms with what we are called to do and what we need to let go of is essential. Releasing those things that we were never meant to carry frees up internal energy and resources to tackle our main calling.

Taking on more than we are called to do speaks to our need for control as much as taking on too little speaks to our fear of failure. Many well-intentioned people throw themselves into their task and try to make a difference, only to come to a gradual halt as they get stuck. Often they start running out of steam as their passion diminishes, and they can't understand what is happening. An undefined calling without boundaries is never sustainable. When we embrace our specific call with clear boundaries, the passion and energy can return. Elijah ended up in the cave of self-pity and isolation in part because he had taken on more than God had given him. His post-cave experience

THE MORE WE RUN from our issues, the more they affect our destiny.

required him to clarify his calling and release control over certain responsibilities that were not his to carry.

STICKING POINT SEVEN:
DEFERRED BEGINNINGS

The final sticking point is deferred beginnings. The time comes when a person needs to say goodbye to the safety of the cave and launch into the risky world of faith living. Elijah's best days were still ahead of him. He had to act decisively and not postpone taking the first step into this new season of his life. All of us come to a point where we know we must take the next step forward or remain stuck. This is a scary moment, the instant we release our grip and choose to trust our heavenly Father.

When my daughter, Marissa, was about four years old she got her head stuck between two metal bars of a stair railing. It happened on a Sunday morning at a grade school we were renting for our church services. I was busy talking to people when an usher pulled me aside with urgency in his voice and said, "Your wife needs you immediately." He added, "Your daughter is stuck."

I rushed toward the hallway, not knowing what to expect. When I turned the corner there she was. Like a prisoner with each little hand grasping a metal bar and her head sticking out between them. I could tell by the look on my wife's face that she was trying to remain calm, but she was holding back tears.

I tried to smile as I asked my daughter, "What's going on, young lady?"

Marissa looked up at me with her big brown eyes and said, "Daddy, I'm stuck."

My wife whispered to me that they had been trying to get her head out without hurting her for a while, but they hadn't made any progress. She tried to coax my daughter to raise her head, but Marissa was afraid of getting hurt. Some of the ushers tried to lift her to get her out, but she was afraid and resisted, clinging to the bars. They tried to pull the bars apart, but they were sturdy iron rods. My wife was so worried she wanted to call the firemen or police. She was already asking how they would manage to cut through the metal without hurting our little girl.

I turned around and gave my daughter a big smile. "Daddy is going to figure how to get you unstuck." I tried to make her relax by telling her that Grandma was going to laugh at this story when I told her later. I teased her that she reminded me of a monkey in the zoo with her head through the bars. She managed to smile. Talking and smiling the whole time, I started to lift her body.

At first she was tense and clung to the bars. "Daddy, it's going to hurt." I assured her that I would be gentle and stop if it hurt. Slowly she stopped resisting and let go of the bars. When she stopped clutching the bars I was able to gently lift her. After several tries her head moved into just the right position and I pulled her out—much to the delight of the growing crowd of spectators. The whole crowd clapped and cheered. But nothing is more rewarding than the hug of a little girl who thinks you are a hero.

I was able to get my daughter unstuck when she finally

trusted me and loosened her grasp. She could have escaped her bars much sooner if she had just let go, but her fear kept her from releasing her grip.

THE DEFINING MOMENT

Most of us reach a point when we have to decide whether we will continue to cling to our security or step out of our cave. This is a defining moment. It involves a step of obedience, an act of faith, trusting our heavenly Father. You will know clearly if you have taken this step or not. I have met many people who know what they should do but live their life in perpetual postponement. They deceive themselves into thinking that they are on the way but actually they are stuck waiting for the right timing, resources, or change in circumstances.

In the next few chapters we will take a look at the process of getting unstuck. For every sticking point there is a step that must be taken to move forward. Understanding why we get stuck is only the beginning. Being willing to work through the process of getting unstuck is what separates those who remain trapped and those who move to their next season.

CHAPTER 4

BREAK OUT OF ISOLATION

Her name was Muyena. I will never forget her gorgeous dark brown eyes or round face, the squeeze of her arms around my neck, and the way she looked at me.

A few years ago I was invited to travel to Mozambique, Africa, to explore mission opportunities. The effects of colonization, a brutal civil war, political unrest, and severe epidemics of malaria and HIV have devastated this beautiful country and resilient people. We visited several orphanages populated by the children of parents who met an early death because of these diseases. We were told that the average life expectancy in Mozambique was about forty-five years.

This particular orphanage was situated on the outskirts of the city of Maputo. It had been built within feet of one of the largest garbage dumps of the city. The Sisters of Charity, the order founded by Mother Teresa of Calcutta, ran this orphanage. Over two hundred children lived within the walls of the compound, but each day the workers fed over four hundred children. The nuns greeted us with a smile while surrounded by dozens of curious African children. Many of these children had never seen white people and were fascinated by the hair on our arms and the color of our skin.

The sisters gave us a hurried tour of their ministry. They pulled back the curtain from one doorway and ushered us into a large dimly lit room that was full of cots with sickly looking men. They informed us that these men were all dying and it was their job to help them die with dignity. They took us to another room of equal size full of women on their deathbed. Many of these women were the mothers of the children we had met earlier. Most were extremely thin and fragile, and clearly struggling for their life.

While we were still gripped by what we had just seen, the tour-guide nun led us to another room. This room was filled wall to wall with cribs. Each crib contained a child under the age of two. As we entered the room a busy nun looked up just long enough to give us a nod as she attended to an infant. I glanced at the crib in front of me and there she was, Muyena, staring up at me. I asked the nun if I could pick up the little girl and hold her for a minute. She seemed reluctant. With a heavy accent she hesitantly said, "You may go ahead. But just be ready."

When I picked up Muyena she immediately wrapped her little legs around my torso, put her arms around my neck and buried her head in my chest. Occasionally she would peek up at me as she held me tight. I spoke to her in soft tones, as I had to my own children when they were babies. She obviously did not understand a word of English, but that didn't bother her one bit. I walked around with her for a few minutes until our tour nun gently insisted we needed to move on. When I attempted to pull Muyena's arms off my neck I realized how strong that little girl was. She clung to me as hard as her little arms and legs could hold her. When I finally placed her back in her crib she let out a wail that made all the children stop and look. Her mouth was wide open as she cried with all her little lungs could muster, but her eyes were fixed on me. It was hard to walk out of that room knowing those tears were calling out to me.

The nun looked at me and said, "Everyone wants to be held by someone."

She lamented that they were too shorthanded to hold the babies much. "All we need is someone to care enough to help hold the babies."

I was so moved I told her I was going back to Chicago, and just as soon as I could I would send a group just to hold the babies. A few months later several ladies from our church flew to Africa to engage in their baby-holding ministry.

I have often thought about that little girl, Muyena, and her determination to be held. That

IT WAS HARD to walk out of that room knowing that baby's tears were calling out to me.

African nun was absolutely right: "Everyone wants to be held by someone." It didn't matter that little Muyena was surrounded by dozens of other babies in that crowded nursery or that she could see the nuns moving about the room. She wanted someone to hold her.

BOWLING ALONE

Orphan babies in Africa are not the only ones that long for personal connection. In cities like Chicago you can be surrounded by people, competing for parking spaces, crowding into elevators, bumping into strangers on sidewalks, and living with very little space between you and your neighbors yet still feel strangely alone. You can be a stay-at-home-mom with children clinging to your housecoat, a college student with two thousand Twitter followers, a doctor who sees dozens of patients a day, or a bus driver who interacts with hundreds of people every shift and still feel isolated. In fact, the most painful loneliness is the kind we experience when people surround us. Most people living in crowded Chicago condos rarely know their next-door neighbors. They share walls, hallways, elevators, and a common building address but remain strangely isolated from each other. Loneliness is not due to the absence of people but to the lack of authentic connection with people.

THE URGE TO ISOLATE

Look closely at the story of Elijah and you will notice that for three years leading up to his crisis of faith, he appears very isolated. He was on the run from authorities and undoubtedly had to hide his identity from his neighbors, which I'm sure didn't help. He was forced to live in a sparsely populated area away from his family and friends. On top of that, when Jezebel threatened him he flees and abandons the only person who has been at his side, his assistant.

He traveled from Jezreel, located in the valley between Mount Carmel and the Sea of Galilee, to the southern city of Beersheba a distance of about one hundred miles. After leaving his assistant, he further isolated himself by traveling to the most remote place he could find. He wasted no time before setting out on another hike into the desert. Elijah's goal was to get as far as he possibly could from everyone he knew. Scripture says, "Elijah was afraid and ran for his life. When he came to Beersheba in Judah, he left his servant there, while he himself went a day's journey into the wilderness" (1 Kings 19:3–4).

Harvard professor Robert Putnam wrote a book called *Bowling Alone: The Collapse and Revival of American Community*, in which he documents the decline in community life over the last five decades. The title of the book came from Putnam's observation of bowling leagues. He discovered that the way we bowl is a microcosm of how we live. Although the number of people who bowl has increased in the last twenty years, the number of people who bowl in leagues has decreased. The percentage of adults who belong to bowling leagues today is only about one quarter of what it was in the 1960s. That statistic alone might just be saying something about bowling. But here are other confirming statistics:

▶ The percentage of people who volunteer in a political campaign—stuffing envelopes, making phone calls, going door-to-door—is today about half what it was in the late 1960s.

▶ In the late 1970s, the average American entertained friends at home about fourteen times a year. Today that number is more like eight.

▶ The percentage of active membership in local clubs and organizations, like PTA, is half what it was in the 1970s.

People are visiting one another less frequently and having friends over less frequently. In short, every objective measurement of participation in community is declining.

Trend forecaster and marketing consultant Faith Popcorn (yes, that's her real name) first used the word "cocooning" in the 1990s. Cocooning is the name given to the trend of people retreating into their homes and socializing less and less face-to-face. When Popcorn predicted this trend, she could not have understood how quickly technology would make cocooning easier than ever before. Our connectivity has increased through Twitter, texting, Facebook, Instagram, Snapchat, and the newest connecting app, but our sense of belonging seems to be at an all-time low. We have created a culture in which people are hyper connected but oddly alone.

Feelings of loneliness have doubled: 40 percent of adults in two recent surveys said they were lonely, up from 20 percent in the 1980s.[1] A study by the American Council of Life Insurance reported that the loneliest group in America is college students. Surrounded by people their own age and busy with an unending slew of activities and interaction, behind closed doors they admit their extreme loneliness. In fact, college students rank as lonelier than divorced people, welfare recipients, single mothers, rural students, housewives, and the elderly.[2]

Concert attendance has been slowly declining over the last ten years, because people no longer want to go to concerts to get lost in a crowd.[3] But if you track an-

OUR CONNECTIVITY has increased, but our sense of belonging seems to be at an all-time low.

other trend over the past ten years, you'll see concerts down but coffeehouses are up. About a year ago the *State Journal* ran a piece on coffeehouses. Listen to what one person had to say: "I come here because I like an atmosphere of busyness. I don't like to feel like I'm alone."[4]

Isolation and insulation are major issues afflicting our culture. They are also major forces driving many to the caves.

Isolation

Isolation has to do with getting away from people and insulation has to do with protecting and shielding ourselves from people. Elijah stepped away from the people in his relational support system when he needed them most. In his effort to get alone he walked right into the sting of loneliness. I have been to the very desert that Elijah walked through and I'm amazed that anyone could survive that rugged, barren wasteland for very long. The desert landscape outside of ancient Beersheba goes as far as the naked eye can see. It stretches in a seemingly endless panorama of rocky, arid, rugged hills. It is part of one of the largest desert landscapes in the world, but the desert is not the only place that we escape into isolation.

Often we are surrounded by people yet we create our own version of the desert, just like my friend Chuck did.

He looked at me with sadness in his eyes and said, "I just don't want to be around people anymore." I had known Chuck since our teen years. He had always been an outgoing, fun-loving extrovert. Most gatherings he was surrounded by people listening to his latest humorous story. People loved him and he loved being around people. The last time I had spoken to Chuck, however, he admitted that he was going through a tough time dealing with criticism at his job. He had been forced to make tough decisions concerning some people that were in conflict. His actions resulted in losing friendships and some of those disgruntled people began to criticize him privately. He found himself in meeting after meeting dealing with volatile people and seeking to mediate peaceful solutions.

For several months Chuck was forced to deal with tense meetings, disgruntled coworkers, and verbal assaults. He began to wear down emotionally and physically. A few months after I had seen Chuck, his wife called me, concerned about his state of mind.

"He is just not the same," she confided. "When he comes home from work he goes in the bedroom and locks the door. We haven't gone out with friends for months. When people call, he doesn't answer the phone. I can't get him out of the house. And worst of all he has shut me out of his world."

Chuck reluctantly agreed to meet with me at an outdoor café. After I asked a few probing questions he finally admitted, "I have been so beaten up by people who I thought were my friends that I just don't have the energy to deal with anyone these days." He confessed that he would cross the street if he saw people he knew walking toward him. I challenged him to take some steps to break out of his seclusion for the sake of his wife and his own sanity. He simply shook his head and said, "You don't understand. I don't have the energy right now to be around people." Even though Chuck was still breathing, I walked away from our coffee meeting feeling like I had experienced the death of a friend.

Unfortunately Chuck's refusal to break isolation ended up costing him his job, his finances, his health, his spiritual life, and nearly his family. Chuck spiraled into such a depression that he could no longer function at work. After being fired from his job he became even more bitter, cynical, and isolated. The next time I saw Chuck again he was merely a shell of the man he had once been. That fun-loving, outgoing, and spiritually vibrant leader had turned into a cynical, negative, despondent introvert living in virtual seclusion.

I have noticed in my own life that when I am doing well I am drawn to open and honest relationships. But when I am struggling, my tendency is to avoid people altogether. Most of us will wrestle with the "Chuck Syndrome" during certain seasons in our life. Like Chuck, we tend to withdraw from people in the midst of our personal crisis when we actually need others the most.

There is a difference between the spiritual discipline of solitude and unhealthy isolation. Wayne Cordeiro, author of *Leading on Empty*, says, "Solitude is a healthy and prescriptive discipline; isolation is a symptom of emotional depletion."[5] Author Hara Estroff, editor of *Psychology Today*, observes this difference between solitude and isolation:

> From the outside, solitude and loneliness look a lot alike. Both are characterized by solitariness. But all resemblance ends at the surface. Loneliness is a negative state, marked by a sense of isolation. One feels that something is missing. It is possible to be with people and still feel lonely—perhaps the most bitter form of loneliness. Solitude is the state of being alone without being lonely.
>
> Solitude is a time that can be used for reflection, inner searching or growth or enjoyment of some kind. Deep reading requires solitude, so does experiencing the beauty of nature. Thinking and creativity usually do too. Solitude is refreshing; an opportunity to renew ourselves. In other words, it replenishes us.
>
> Loneliness is harsh, punishment, a deficiency state, a state of discontent marked by a sense of estrangement, an awareness of excess aloneness.[6]

Isolation is the consequence of retreating from those whose help we need in times of trouble.

Insulation

Isolation is the first of two critical errors we can make when we face difficult life challenges. The second is insulation. Isolation leads us to get away from people, but insulation drives us to protect and shield ourselves from people. The first account of any human insulating himself is found in the book of Genesis. When Adam and Eve were healthy, they craved community and relationship with God and each other. As soon as their world was shattered by a blatant act of disobedience, relationships and community changed forever. Suddenly Adam and Eve needed to cover up from each other and hide from God. They hid when they heard the sound of God in the garden. Notice how Adam behaved: "But the Lord God called to the man, 'Where are you?' He answered, 'I heard you in the garden, and I was afraid because I was naked; so I hid'" (Genesis 3:9–10).

What drove the first couple to insulate themselves was the fear and shame they felt. Fear of rejection and shame over our own failures are natural insulators. When Adam and Eve needed God and each other the most, their natural counterproductive reflex was to isolate and insulate. It is a strange paradox that at our point of greatest need most of us tend to hide from our greatest resource—relationships.

Elijah walked through the desert of isolation for forty days and traveled two hundred miles in absolute silence and solitude. The desert can do strange things to your mind. For almost a month, he walked alone talking to himself, letting the fear-filled thoughts flood his mind. Scholars estimate that the journey would take roughly twenty days of ordinary walking, plus climbing the jagged seven thousand feet to the peak of Mount Sinai. However, it took Elijah forty days. Likely, the sluggish effect of discouragement and dejection made him drag his feet. I picture Elijah preoccupied with his thoughts, mumbling to himself, and rehearsing his story over and over as he slowly drags his feet toward Mount Horeb. By the time he reached the cave, he was showing the destructive effects of too much time alone.

BREAKING OUT OF ISOLATION

When God began drawing Elijah out of his cave, He was not only preparing Elijah to exit the spiritual prison he had been stuck in. He was also equipping him to enter into a new season of healthy relationships. God gave Elijah a specific plan for breaking his history of isolation. This relational plan included: a confidant, colleagues, and a community. When Elijah entered the cave he was lonely and isolated. When he exited he had a plan to break out of isolation.

IT IS A STRANGE paradox that at the point of our greatest need, most of us tend to hide from our greatest resource— relationships.

Fast-forward and you can hear God commanding Elijah to return the way he had come to his cave. "When you get there," God continued, "anoint Hazael king over Aram. Also, anoint Jehu son of Nimshi king over Israel, and anoint Elisha son of Shaphat from Abel Meholah to succeed you as prophet" (1 Kings 19:15–16).

Breaking out of isolation and choosing the vulnerability of connectedness is part of the post-cave restoration process. Elijah had become accustomed to working solo on his mission. Part of God's post-cave solution was to provide an apprentice to accompany and succeed Elijah. Elijah was to spend a lot of time in his new season in the company of young Elisha.

Two things would happen as a result: a new leader was being shaped and an older leader was being restored.

To get unstuck we need to understand the importance of healthy relationships in our life and work. Elijah emerged from his cave determined to put three new relational spheres in place. He stepped out with a confidant, a community, and a plan to engage his colleagues.

Colleagues are partners who help carry the load of responsibility in our life. Elijah didn't have a close relationship with his new colleagues, Hazael and Nimshi, but he did ask them to take responsibility for areas of ministry that he could not handle.

A confidant can take on various forms, but all forms require a close, trusting relationship. Elijah's closest relationship was with Elisha, his apprentice and eventual successor. Elisha was Elijah's confidant, close companion, and day-to-day assistant. The prophet poured his time, experience, and his very life into his young protégé. This is what we at New Life call life-on-life impartation.

Finally, Elijah stepped out of his cave with a new understanding of his community. One of the issues that led him to the cave in the first place was wrongly assuming that he was alone in his values and convictions. He believed he was the only faithful Israelite in all the land. God revealed to Elijah that, in fact, there were seven thousand others in Israel who had not bowed their knee to Baal. He discovered that he was part of a much larger community that shared his views, a community he was unaware even existed. God's design for a healthy new season in Elijah's life involved discovering his colleagues, his confidant, and his community.

DREADING MONDAYS?

Many people dread Monday morning. I love it. Every Monday morning I come together with an amazing group of colleagues, confidants, and a community that travel from around the city. We call them the New Life Pastoral Team. We pray, worship, share, learn, and celebrate life and ministry together. I have been with some of these leaders for over two decades. We have battle scars to show and shared mountaintops we have conquered together. We have traveled together, prayed over each other's children, cried together, laughed to the point of tears together, challenged one another, confronted one another, fasted and prayed and shared life together. It is hard for me to imagine surviving the challenges of ministry in the city without this team.

Working with people in tough neighborhoods in cities like Chicago can be brutal. The turnover rate among pastors, counselors, social workers, and law enforcement is high. Burnout is a widespread problem. Many people become so overwhelmed with the immensity of the needs and intensity of the problems that they quit or they harden themselves to the point that they simply go through the motions in their jobs. A small minority discovers the power of healthy relationships. I am convinced that the leaders who survive long-term are those who intentionally build or find enduring community.[7]

The healthy "long-termers" that maintain their sanity, enjoy healthy marriages, and still love their job are those who have discovered the three relational spheres that God revealed to Elijah.

In his book *Boundaries for Leaders*, Henry Cloud summarizes the Second Law of Thermodynamics: "Everything in the universe is running down, running out of energy, and becoming less organized." He applies this law to people and their relational health. People will also run down, run out of energy, and become less focused if they have no input. He points out that in a closed system, where there is no relational input, this running out of energy is inevitable, but in an open system this process can be reversed. Dr. Cloud encourages his readers to "set a boundary on your tendency to be a 'closed system' and open yourself up to outside inputs that bring you energy and guidance."[8]

Maybe as you read this chapter you realized that you are living in isolation, but you are wondering what you can do to break out. I encourage you to start with three simple steps. First, start with what you already have. You may already have friends in your inner circle who would make great confidants. List your three closest friends. Have a conversation with each of them and explore what it would take to get together once a month. Make your meetings informal and transparent and give each other permission to ask the hard questions.

Second, think of a few people that work or volunteer with you. Do you have some colleagues you can share responsibility with? Do you have coworkers you can partner with to help you grow and learn from each other? These relationships will not be as personal as your relationship with your confidants, but they can be very supportive.

Third, take a step to invest in a community of faith. Find a local church you can join and in which you can use your gifts and talents to help make a difference. Fight the urge to be critical or think that no one else is like you. Roll up your sleeves and find a place to serve and be on mission together.

This past week my wife received a card from one of her friends that is part of our leadership team:

Dee, It's been on my mind to send you a thank-you card for a while. You have been by my side every dark step of the way through my anxiety. Knowing that you were just a phone call away, ready to read Scripture to me and pray for me, was a huge comfort. Thank you for being there for me each and every morning and for speaking truth to me when irrational fears threatened to take over. It means a lot to know that you went through your own season of fear and anxiety and that you've learned how to give those fears to God and train your mind to quickly move on from fear to truth. Thank you for praying me through and never losing hope for my future.

The power of a friend is irreplaceable. We don't realize how much we need community until we go through our dark seasons. It is in those moments that we realize isolation is not broken by simply waiting for life to change. Isolation is overcome when we take steps to lower our guard, open our life, and invite others to the journey.

CHAPTER 5

RETHINK YOUR THINKING

I was a pastor in my twenties in over my head. I knew I needed help, so I called Jake, my former college roommate, and asked him to move to Chicago and join me. I knew that he had a calling on his life and a sincere passion for God. Jake was very gifted and eager to serve, but he struggled with the voices from his past. He grew up in a broken household with parents who fought through multiple divorces. The scars of dysfunction manifested in Jake in a hypersensitive conscience and a sense of inadequacy that bombarded him with guilt and accusations any time he stepped into new opportunities.

Jake started out with enthusiasm in his new ministry role. But soon he began to experience unhealthy guilt and chronic feelings of condemnation. Jake and I had long talks about his struggle but nothing seemed to be helping. After several months the pressure was more than he could bear. Unannounced he packed up his little grey Ford Escort and tried to escape Chicago. On his way out of the city he was struck with a sudden pain in his side that forced him to pull the car to the side of the road. Sensing God was trying to get his attention, but determined to run anyway, he made his way onto the expressway and drove about forty-five minutes outside of Chicago when his car abruptly broke down. He managed to turn the car around and barely made it back to the city. The mechanic that looked at his engine commented, "It must have been God that kept this car running, because this engine is shot." Jake returned to Chicago discouraged and disappointed.

Often what drives us to the paralyzing cave of isolation, frustration, and fear are the voices in our head that speak to us about our identity and destiny. The message becomes a script that we repeat to ourselves like a bad recording, over and over, until it becomes our new reality. This is what happened to Jake. Maybe that's what happened to you.

HOW DID YOU GET TO YOUR CAVE?

Elijah had traveled nearly two hundred miles in solitude before he reached the cave. He stepped into the darkness of the cave exhausted and must have quickly fallen asleep.

Elijah wakes up. He is in pitch darkness. The air is damp and cold. His body aches all over. His eyes search the dark in vain for some familiar reminder; it takes him a few seconds to remember where he is. His eyes start to adjust. Then, like a flood, the memories come rushing back. His heart sinks as he remembers he is a fugitive on the run with a contract on his head. He is in a cave. This cave is his new home.

About that time he hears a familiar voice. He has heard it before, and he knows immediately who it is. The question breaks the silence and comes loud and clear.

"What are you doing here, Elijah?"

I don't like to be asked questions when I just wake up from a deep sleep. I need a cup of coffee and a few minutes to myself. But Elijah wakes up to a probing question that requires profound soul-searching and self-examination to answer.

"What are you doing here, Elijah?"

But instead of reflecting on the question, Elijah offers a quick and well-rehearsed answer. His answer gives us a first-hand look at his thinking. We get a glimpse at the negative script that had been replaying over and over in Elijah's mind during his long walk in the desert. He blurts out what he has been waiting to say for a long time: "I have been very zealous for the Lord God Almighty. The Israelites have rejected your covenant, torn down your altars, and put your prophets to death with the sword. I am the only one left, and now they are trying to kill me too" (1 Kings 19:10).

Every person stuck must answer this question: "What am I doing here?" To answer this question you will have to rewind and remember what drove you to this place in the first place. As you rewind your story, you will naturally focus on the difficult circumstances and challenging people, but the real focus should be on your thinking. What drives us to the cave is not the people or circumstances but rather our faulty thinking.

Can you hear the frustration, discouragement, and self-pity in Elijah's response?

Pointing to how unfair life has been and how hard we have

tried is a common knee-jerk reaction to the question, "What are you doing here?" Elijah was convinced that cave dwelling was not his choice but rather the inevitable consequence of circumstances outside his control. Through his answer we discover that he is driven by his failed effort, his disappointment in others, his loneliness, and a pessimistic view of the future.

Clearly, when the all-knowing God of the universe asks a question, it is not because He doesn't know the answer. When Almighty God asks a question it's because He wants you to discover something in the process of wrestling to find your answer.

> **EVERY PERSON** stuck must answer this question: "What am I doing here?"

Just before Jesus performed one of His most astounding miracles, He turned to one of His disciples and asked him the same kind of question. At the end of a long day of teaching, Jesus looked up and saw a crowd of people following Him. Everyone was tired and hungry, and it was nearing dinnertime. Jesus turned to His disciple Philip and asked, "Where shall we buy bread for these people to eat?" (John 6:5).

What I love about this passage is that it tells us exactly why Jesus asked this question: "to test him, for he already had in mind what he was going to do" (v. 6). Jesus had a plan but He still asked the question. He didn't need a brainstorm session with Philip and the disciples to come up with a creative solution. He wasn't stuck and needing logistical advice. He already had a strategy, but He was testing Philip and probing his heart.

Philip thought for a minute and began doing some culinary mathematics. He put on his caterer hat and calculated how they might provide supper for five thousand hungry men. The more he thought the more he began to panic. Philip responded, a little exasperated, "It would take more than half a year's wages to buy enough bread for each one to have a bite!" (John 6:7).

I can just hear Philip: "Jesus, feeding these men would cost us a small fortune. Even if our treasurer, Judas, could come up with the money, where would we find a bakery open at this time? If we did convince a baker to help us, it would take days to make that much bread. Supposing a bakery was able to provide thousands of loaves of bread, we would need to figure out how to transport the meals. By the time we got the bread to these hungry people, it would be breakfast time again. No disrespect, Jesus, but trying to feed these people is just crazy."

Philip's response revealed what Jesus already knew. His disciples still had a lot to learn about trusting Him. Jesus was setting the stage for one of the most talked-about multiplication miracles in all of history. He already knew that a little boy would offer to share his lunch with the crowd. He already knew that He would distribute a child's lunch to His disciples and ask them to feed over five thousand hungry men, plus women and children, until they were full. He already knew that they would collect twelve baskets full of leftover lunch. When he asked Philip, "Where shall we buy bread for these people to eat?" He already had a clear plan.

Similarly, when God asked Elijah "What are you doing here?" He knew the answer and already had a plan.

THE VICTIM MINDSET

One of the most common forms of distorted thinking is a victim mentality. Elijah had developed a bad case of victim thinking. You will inevitably stay stuck when you start believing that you are a victim and that you are not responsible for the cave you are stuck in.

She sat there with her arms crossed and her body turned slightly away from her husband. He faced me but he kept glancing, frustrated, over at his wife. Suddenly he blurted out, "When she starts respecting me and supporting me then I will start loving her the way she is asking me to." He paused. "How can I 'nurture' her when she is constantly nagging me and fighting every single decision I make!"

She spun around and snapped, "I can't change until he changes. I can't respect a man who doesn't treat a woman the way she deserves to be treated." She glared at him. "When you start listening to me and putting me first as your wife, then I will show you respect. Until then I cannot respect you."

He was demanding respect and she was demanding love.

"Let me get this straight," I interrupted. "Neither of you can change until the other changes first?"

I have had this conversation many times with people stuck in a relational stalemate. The frustrated husband thinks, *I'm going to continue to work all the overtime I can and make excuses to be out until my wife changes her attitude.* The wife thinks, *I'm going to continue to nag him until he starts coming home earlier and proving that he cares about me and our family.* Both spouses believe they are victims and unless the other person makes a move first they cannot make a positive move either. This mindset makes us a victim to someone else's mood swings and decisions. Many of us sit in our cave waiting for someone else to change before we make a move.

Elijah had started to operate under that same distorted thinking. During his journey to the cave he began to point to his difficult circumstances and to the wrongs of the people to justify moping in his dark, damp prison.

It is true that we cannot control what people do against us. We have little power over other people's attitude and behavior toward us. But we can always choose whether or not we take on a victim mentality. Look at Elijah's response a little more closely.

Elijah felt like he had been faithful to the Lord, but no one else was. How is that his fault? Of course Elijah was not responsible for the actions of other people. But he was responsible for his own response to their actions.

MANY OF US SIT in our cave waiting for someone else to change before we make a move.

As a father you are not responsible for the rebellious attitude of your teenage son, but you are responsible for your harshness and anger toward him. As a wife, you are not responsible for the insensitivity and thoughtlessness of your husband, but you are responsible for the bitterness and resentment you allow to grow in your heart. As an employee, you are not responsible for the bad choices your bosses make in the workplace, but you are responsible for the critical outlook you allow to rob your energy and productivity. As a daughter-in-law, you are not responsible for the controlling insecurity of your mother-in-law, but you are responsible for how you allow anger to influence your reactions. As a college student, you are not responsible for the nasty divorce your parents are going through, but you are responsible for the lack of forgiveness you allow to invade your life. As a boss you are not responsible for the negative antimanagement attitude of certain employees, but you are responsible for your dismissive or harsh reactions to them.

Elijah could not be held responsible for the spiritual hardness and falling away of Israel, but he was responsible for giving up hope and no longer trusting God in the crisis. For three years Elijah fought to maintain the right attitude in the face of challenging circumstances—and succeeded. Ironically, by losing confidence in God, Elijah became just like the other Israelites whom he blamed for his condition.

It is obvious that Elijah had rehearsed this distorted message over and over. When God asks him the second time, "What are you doing here, Elijah?" Elijah automatically answers exactly the same way: "I have been very zealous for the Lord God Almighty. The Israelites have rejected your covenant, torn down your altars, and put your prophets to death with the sword. I am the only one left, and now they are trying to kill me too" (1 Kings 19:13–14).

This script has become his automatic reflex response.

It is one thing to fall into occasional distorted thinking, but it takes a personal toll when we get stuck there.

THE TRIGGER POINT

The term "trigger point" was coined in 1942 by physician and medical researcher Dr. Janet Travell to describe a painful point in the human body that, when touched, triggers a twitch response or pain in another part of the body.

The thinking that drives most of us to our caves is gradual and progressive, but it usually has a "trigger point" that, when touched, causes a reaction in another part of our life. Up until the Mount Carmel contest, Elijah appears to be almost superhuman. He is unflinching before the threats of a king. He stands defiantly, with nerves of steel, on Mount Carmel. He believes God without wavering. But then it happens. Elijah snaps and begins spiraling downward at high velocity.

Fear invaded his thinking and he couldn't shake it: "Elijah was afraid and ran for his life." You may have been doing great for years when, like Elijah, your trigger point is touched. Your wife mentions divorce, you find pot in your teenage son's backpack, your employer hands out pink slips, you are diagnosed with cancer, a trusted leader disappoints you. A trigger point can unleash a flood of negative emotion that inundates your thinking and drowns your hope.

A few years ago I experienced a trigger event that affected me firsthand. My healthy cousin in her late twenties was diagnosed with a brain tumor. She was a brave young woman who battled the enemy of cancer with strong faith and determination. After a valiant courageous fight she died on her thirtieth birthday. I remember feeling for the first time how short and frail life is. Shortly after, I began having aches and pains in my lower back. I consulted a doctor but he could not find the problem. I asked for further testing but he did not think it was warranted. I dismissed the intermittent pain without giving much thought to it.

Then one day I was asked to visit the hospital where an older friend of mine was on his deathbed in a coma. I was there for less than thirty minutes when his monitor stopped beeping and he passed away. His son was irate. He explained that his father had been complaining of lower back pain for months but the doctors had been slow to order tests that could have identified much sooner the cancer that had killed him. He described the pain that his father was having—pain that started in his back and made its way around to his side. He was describing the exact pain I had been experiencing for the past few months! My mind raced as I drove away from the hospital. I called to ensure my life insurance policy was up-to-date. When I got home I hugged my wife tighter than usual. I went into my office and wrote a letter leaving instructions to my family to be read after my death. I began to envision my funeral and pictured my wife as a distraught widow. I went back to the doctor and insisted on further testing.

A TRIGGER POINT can unleash a flood of negative emotion that inundates your thinking and drowns your hope.

A few days later the doctor called me back. I braced myself for the bad news. "Mr. Jobe," he said, "I'm not sure how we missed it the first time around, but I'm sorry to tell you that you have a serious kidney infection." The doctor was surprised at how happy I was to hear that news. I wanted to dance around my office singing, "I have a kidney infection. I'm so happy!" I was so relieved it wasn't cancer. I spent several days in the hospital fighting the infection, but I have never been so happy to be sick.

If you have never experienced a serious trigger event it may seem irrational, but fear is never rational. Elijah's normally confident demeanor and solid faith had been shaken. The noise of fear-filled thinking became so loud in Elijah's head that this legendary man of God melted. One threat from the powerful queen Jezebel opened the floodgates of fear.

THE LOUDEST MESSAGE WINS

Whatever message is repeated the most and the loudest in your head will determine your reflex response to life. The more time we spend alone with our negative or distorted thoughts, the more real and entrenched they become in our thinking. People who spend too much time isolated from healthy interaction often become convinced of their own delusions and distorted thoughts.

But there is hope.

RESTART YOUR THINKING

Although Jake attempted to run from Chicago he ended up right back where he began and was forced to reexamine his own journey. He had to wrestle with the same question Elijah wrestled with.

"What am I doing here?"

Jake determined it was time to stop running. It was time to work on hearing the voice of God over the voice of guilt. He committed to do everything possible to reboot his thinking.

Jake began the painful process of reviewing the journey that led him to his cave. He revisited the deep-rooted hurts and issues he had been running from. One day while walking and praying in a local park he opened up his fist and released the people who had hurt him deeply. With his palm stretched open before God, he committed to not hold on to the hurt any more. He began to carry with him Scripture written on note cards, passages that spoke of the promises of God and Jake's own identity in Christ. Every time he heard the voice of guilt and condemnation, he quickly pulled out a card and started reading until the negative voice was drowned out. For months he carried these cards in his pocket, posted them on his mirror, kept them on the dashboard of his car. In the beginning he had to review them dozens of times each day. Progress was very slow. But with time he discovered he was starting to build an automatic response to the distorted thinking. Each time it surfaced, the grace-filled truth he was meditating on kicked in. Jake will be the first to admit that this process took time and the battle was intense, but in time his thinking was rebooted. Jake has now walked for years as a faith-filled leader without shying away from challenges and opportunities. Turning up the volume of God's voice and turning down the volume of his misguided script was the beginning of a new season.

Have you asked yourself honestly how you ended up stuck in your cave? Your journey out of the cave begins by confronting the thinking that drove you there in the first place. Now is the time to wrestle with the question God is whispering to you: "What are you doing here?"

CHAPTER 6

TURN UP THE GOD VOLUME

Celebrated film producer Jeffrey Katzenberg asked, "What does God sound like?" I was in Hollywood at the production headquarters of DreamWorks. Twenty other evangelical pastors and I had been invited to preview the film *The Prince of Egypt* and offer our feedback. I felt a little out of place as the youngest pastor there, and in the company of nationally known church leaders. They invited me as a representative of the "younger generation."

The project was impressive. The film told the story of the life of Moses and his journey from slave to liberator of Israel. It took one million individual drawings to make the eighty-eight-minute animated feature. The film went on to gross $218 million worldwide in theaters. Behind the scenes, two hundred theologians and religious workers were brought to Hollywood to offer their opinions of Moses and the story being told.

From his seat in the DreamWorks conference room, Katzenberg described the team's most difficult task in creating the epic film. "We had a hard time knowing how to record the voice of God in the burning bush scene," he explained. "We considered the thunder voice approach and the deep baritone, 'James Earl Jones' style, but in the end none of those seem to fit." He paused. "Then we had an idea. We took the voices of a hundred different people—men, women, and children—and recorded them into one single voice track."

God's lines were spoken by all the film's lead actors together. Sound engineer Lon Bender directed the actors to whisper the lines, so that none would dominate the performance. He and his team then took the voice of Val Kilmer, who played the voice of Moses, and made his voice louder than the others. As a result, Kilmer gave voice to both Moses and God suggesting that often we hear God speak to us in our own voice.

The concept of more than a hundred different voices making up the voice of God actually had a prophetic ring to it. Not because God has a hundred different voices but because He has spoken in hundreds of different ways to His people through various means and people.

DO YOU HEAR HIM WHEN HE SPEAKS?

I guess a lot of people, besides film producers in Hollywood have asked themselves the same question over the course of history, "What does God sound like?" from deep spiritual thinkers with grey beards and wrinkled brows to little round-faced children in Sunday school classes.

Of course we can never know, this side of heaven, what God's voice sounds like. But Scripture tells us clearly that God does speak to us. He has spoken through the prophets and through His Word, and most perfectly through His Son, Jesus Christ (Hebrews 1:1–2). The question, then, is not whether God speaks but whether we hear Him when He speaks. If we ever hope to leave our cave, we must learn to recognize the voice of God when He speaks to us.

We cannot hear God's voice clearly or experience His presence personally until we step out of the insulation of our cave. The first question God asked Elijah was, "What are you doing here?" But the first action God asked Elijah to take was "Go out." God called Elijah to step out from the depths of the cave to a place where he could experience the full impact of His presence: "The Lord said, 'Go out and stand on the mountain in the presence of the Lord, for the Lord is about to pass by' " (1 Kings 19:11).

Sometimes we need to reposition ourselves to hear God's voice clearly. Just the other day I was on my cellphone talking with my wife, Dee, when her voice became choppy. I had to walk outside the building to find better reception. If I had stayed deep inside the building, my wife's voice would have continued to be unclear. I had to reposition myself before I could hear her clearly again. God was calling Elijah to reposition himself.

Elijah was instructed to prepare for God's presence by stepping out of the cave and positioning himself for an encounter. The cave represents the dark place where fear-filled thoughts can dominate and isolation can reign supreme. Stepping toward the entrance of the cave shows a willingness on Elijah's part to encounter God. James 4:8 tells us, "Come near to God and he will come near to you. Wash your hands, you sinners, and purify your hearts, you double-minded." Scripture invites us to take a step toward God and assures us that, when we do, He will meet us there. God invited Elijah to meet His presence outside the cave. He called him out toward a fresh encounter with the Presence that could transform him.

Elijah responded with silence. He didn't move a single muscle. Based on his lack of response, you might think Elijah did not hear God. But that was not the case. Elijah heard the voice of God, but he was slow to act in obedience. I suspect that Elijah moved slowly because there were other voices in his head competing with the voice of God, and he was still deciding which voice to listen to.

THE WAKE-UP CALL

So God decided to make some noise. If Elijah would not come when God asked, God was willing to cause a scene. "Then a great and powerful wind tore the mountains apart and shattered the rocks before the Lord, but the Lord was not in the wind. After the wind there was an earthquake, but the Lord was not in the earthquake. After the earthquake came a fire, but the Lord was not in the fire" (1 Kings 19:11–12).

When Elijah refused to move, God sent the equivalent of a tornado past the entrance of the cave. No doubt Elijah could hear the howling of wind and shattering of rocks on the surface of the mountain. As soon as the wind quieted down, the earth began trembling. Elijah could hear the sound of stones falling and the earth moaning as an earthquake violently shook the mountain. When God moves, He cannot be ignored for long.

Can you imagine what it feels like to be in a cave when an earthquake hits?

Beneath the sandstone-capped ridges of Mammoth Cave National Park lies the most extensive cave system on earth, with over four hundred miles of passageways mapped and surveyed. These caves lie 150 miles from the New Madrid Fault, a major earthquake fault line along the Mississippi River. In 1812 the region was shaken by an earthquake that is estimated to have registered 8.7 on the Richter scale. Some miners were working in the caves at the time. One of the miners caught in the cave during the earthquake said, "About five minutes before the shock a heavy rumbling noise was heard coming out of the cave like a mighty gust of wind; when that ceased, the rocks cracked, and all appeared to be going in a moment of final destruction."[1]

SOMETIMES WE need to reposition ourselves to hear God's voice clearly.

I imagine Elijah must have experienced the same effects. He probably started scurrying toward the mouth of the cave as soon as the earth started rumbling. His lethargy quickly turned to an adrenaline rush and his heart must have pounded as dust filled the cave. God had gotten his attention. There is no way that Elijah could continue to ignore the sound of God. When the earthquake stopped, while Elijah was in view of the opening of the cave, God sent fire. The passage makes it sound as if this was not a slow-burning forest fire, but rather a fiery burst that lightened the sky and sent a flash of heat through the entrance to the cave.

Why the wind, earthquake, and fire? Why the divine theatrics? This dramatic display of power and supernatural fireworks was aimed at moving Elijah from the belly of the cave to the entrance. This was God's way of repositioning Elijah for an encounter with His manifest presence.

When we refuse to respond to His voice, God sometimes uses other means to move us along. Jonah refused to go to Nineveh, so God sent a storm and a man-swallowing fish. The population of earth refused to listen in Noah's day, so God sent the flood. Pharaoh refused to listen, so God sent the plagues. Humanity refused to believe so God sent His Son.

Sometimes in the darkness of our cave we need to be awakened by the dramatic sound of God before we can position ourselves for His presence. Scripture makes a point of highlighting the fact that God's presence was not in the earthquake, whirlwind, or fire. "Then a great and powerful wind tore the mountains apart and shattered the rocks before the Lord, but the *Lord was not* in the wind. After the wind there was an earthquake, but the *Lord was not* in the earthquake. After the earthquake came a fire, but the *Lord was not* in the fire" (1 Kings 19:11–12 italics added).

SILENCING WHITE NOISE

The famous nineteenth-century preacher Charles Haddon Spurgeon put it this way:

And now the thunder ceased, and the lightning was gone, and the earth was still, and the wind was hushed, and there was a dead calm, and out of the midst of the still air there came what the Hebrew calls "a voice of gentle silence," as if silence had become audible. There is nothing more terrible than an awful stillness after a dreaded uproar.[2]

Often it is the extraordinary interruptions and dramatic wake-up calls that make us listen attentively. I have heard many stories of people who just before they awakened to the voice of God were startled by the dramatic in their life. A nearly fatal car accident. A difficult and painful divorce. A cancer diagnosis. The collapse of a business venture. The loud, attention-getting sirens are not an end in themselves but merely a warning of what is coming. The flashing lights and siren of the police cars and security vehicles make way for the President's entourage, but the first family is not in the police car. Do not confuse the announcement with the presence.

You have to rewind Elijah's story to discover why he lost touch with the sound of God. Elijah did well until the noise found a foothold, an open door to get inside his head, then he fell apart. In the chapters leading up to 1 Kings 19, Elijah is a model of determination and boldness. When all of his opposition is external, he seems unshakable, a spiritual man of iron. But as soon as the noise gets inside his head, he quickly disintegrates into an emotional basket case.

When I was a young dad, I determined that we would try to eat dinner as a family every evening. Through the teen years it has not always been easy to rally the family and get everyone to the table on time, but we've stayed determined.

Now I understand why in the old cowboy movies the cook would ring a bell to announce the chow was ready. There have been many evenings when I have called upstairs to my now fourteen-year-old son announcing that it is dinnertime only to be met with silence. I once walked by the stairs and called out, "Grant, dinner is ready."

I waited and heard no answer. In a louder voice I said, "Grant, did you hear me? Dinner is ready." Still no answer.

Increasing my volume significantly, I shouted, "Grant! Can you hear me? Dinner is ready!" Still no answer. Then I banged on the wall closest to his room and said loudly, "Can you hear me?" It wasn't an earthquake but it had the same effect.

This time, from inside his upstairs room, I heard Grant ask, "Dad, did you say something?"

A little irritated, I said, "Yes, this is my fourth time calling you. Why aren't you responding?"

"Oh, I had headphones on. I couldn't hear you."

There you have it. The noise in his ears was louder than my voice, so although I was calling to him with good news (dinnertime) he still couldn't hear me. When the voices in our head are louder than the voice of God, we have a problem.

In the New Testament, Paul reminds us about the challenge of keeping the noise out of our heads. He calls us to "be made new in the attitude of your minds; and to put on the new self, created to be like God in true righteousness and holiness." As we do this, it's important that we "do not give the devil a foothold" (Ephesians 4:23–24, 27).

Fear and anger are two of the primary footholds the enemy uses to get noise inside our heads. Anger and fear are irrational emotional cousins that override our logical thinking and, if given the chance, will sabotage our faith as well. For three years Elijah stood up to an egomaniacal king bent on taking his life. But after Elijah's mountaintop experience, where he single-handedly challenged the false religious system of a whole nation, fear and anxiety crept in.

> **ANGER AND FEAR** are irrational emotional cousins that override our logical thinking and, if given the chance, will sabotage our faith as well.

Maybe it was because Elijah thought it would all be over after the showdown on Mount Carmel. That's called unmet expectations. After three years he was tired of hiding, drained from the pressure, and expected his enemies to surrender to God. Instead Jezebel, the wicked queen, became defiant. Her threat of death was the trigger point that sent Elijah spiraling downward.

Psychologist and author Henry Cloud describes this tendency in his book *Boundaries for Leaders*. He emphasizes the fact that leaders need to set boundaries on their tendency to allow single events or results to define them. Sometimes one difficult event can set a domino reaction in motion. We take an event personally, we think it is pervasive, and we think it will be permanent. Cloud describes the conversation we have when fear starts to get a grip in these terms. "Personalizing: 'I am not good enough to pull this off. It's going to be terrible. They won't like me.' Pervasive: 'Everything is going south. Nothing we are doing is working and this will not either.' Permanent: 'It's not going to be any different tomorrow. It will always be the same as it is now.'"[3]

Perhaps you have allowed a trigger event in your life to overwhelm you. Maybe you have allowed an event or incident to open a door that you cannot close. It has become the negative door prop in your life. You don't get the job promotion and fear props the door open. Your boyfriend says it's not going to work out and the anxiety noise gets louder. Your son comes back with a bad report card and the worry volume rises. Whatever message gets a foothold inside your head and is repeated at a high volume will shape your future thinking.

THE SOUND OF GOD

Three chapters into the Bible we find the first record of people responding to the attention-grabbing sound of God before they actually hear His voice. God was looking for Adam and Eve in the garden.

"Then the man and his wife heard the sound of the Lord God as he was walking in the garden in the cool of the day, and they hid from the Lord God among the trees of the garden" (Genesis 3:8).

Notice this verse says they "heard the *sound* of the Lord God as he was walking in the garden." Not the voice of God, but the sound of God. I am not sure what God sounds like when He walks. I do know however, that God can be as loud or as quiet as He wants to be. Clearly God chose to make Himself heard as He walked through the garden that day. He knew what Adam and Eve were hiding and gave them an opportunity to respond to His arrival. He virtually stomps His feet through the garden announcing His presence before He speaks.

But the Lord God called to the man, "Where are you?"

The man answered, "I heard you in the garden, and I was afraid because I was naked; so I hid" (Genesis 3:9–10).

Instead of emerging from their hiding place with arms open wide and admitting their failure, the first couple hid from God's presence driven by guilt, fear, and shame.

When my daughter turned twelve, my wife and I felt comfortable leaving our three kids alone for the evening without a babysitter. Of course, we occasionally would get a call on my cellphone requesting conflict resolution intervention. We received one such call when we were out on a dinner date. My daughter was annoyed with one of her brothers. "Dad, he is not listening to me! I have told him three times to turn off the TV and get ready for bed. He is laughing and saying, 'You are not the boss of me.'"

I could hear her brother in the background saying, "Crybaby. I'm going to tell Dad what you did . . ."

Since I was in the middle of a nice quiet dinner with my wife I told them I would deal with the situation when I got home. Later that evening I arrived home and noticed all the lights still on. When I entered the front door I was a little irritated that our quiet dinner had been interrupted, so I came in extra loud. I wanted them to know Dad had arrived. When I walked in the door, I announced, "I'm home!"

My younger son, the alleged guilty party, did not come to greet me, but of course my daughter met me at the door and immediately began pleading her case. She gave me a full description of what had happened and how disobedient her brother had been and how innocent she was. I had to go looking for the little offender who was simulating sleep in his room with the lights turned off. When I entered the room I knew he had heard the "sound of Dad." His Oscar-worthy "innocent boy sleeping" performance wasn't good enough to fool me. Dad was home and he knew it.

In a similar way, God announces His presence at key times in our life. Not just when it's time to discipline, but when He wants us to hear Him clearly. He stomps His feet, clears His throat, and lets us know God is in the house. His deliberate *sound* is a preparation for His *voice*.

God used His sound—the wind, the earthquake, and the fire—to get Elijah's attention before He spoke.

LISTEN FOR THE WHISPER

After the wind, earthquake, and fire, Elijah was fully awake and listening for what would happen next.

"And after the fire came a gentle whisper. When Elijah heard it, he pulled his cloak over his face and went out and stood at the mouth of the cave" (1 Kings 19:12–13).

Elijah knew instinctively that this was the whisper of God. It wasn't dramatic and loud. There were no lightning bolts and thunder. It was the opposite of the supernatural disasters that had just taken place, but God was in it. The still, small voice was the sound of God leading Elijah to the presence of God. The voice of the Spirit is always a guide to the presence. This time, the gentle voice of God compelled Elijah to cover his head and move toward the presence of Him who spoke.

We recently partnered with an overcrowded public school in our neighborhood to create classroom space for 165 kindergarten children. I am impressed with how well behaved these children are. Last week I walked past twenty-five Chicago kindergarten boys and girls. They were walking in pairs with the teacher at the front of the line. You could have heard a pin drop as they walked the hallway. This veteran teacher had developed a technique to make normally chaotic hallways orderly and quiet. All the children walked with their hands clasped together and their two index fingers over their lips, which reminded them that this was a no-talking and no-touching zone. The only voice I heard was the voice of the teacher quietly giving them instructions.

GOD'S CHILDREN hunger for a continual conversation with God.

At times, chaos and confusion will overwhelm us unless we learn how to silence the voices, put a finger over our lips, and hear only the holy whisper as we walk the hallways of life quietly toward His presence.

There is a small booklet that spoke to me profoundly as a college student. Brother Lawrence, author of *The Practice of the Presence of God*, was a Carmelite monk who worked in the kitchen at the monastery where he served. Lawrence wrote, "There is not in the world a kind of life more sweet and delightful than that of a continual conversation with God. Those only can comprehend it who practice and experience it; yet I do not advise you to do it from that motive. It is not pleasure which we ought to seek in this exercise; but let us do it from a principle of love, and because God would have us."[4]

God's children hunger for this presence, this continual conversation with God. We cannot manipulate an encounter with God. We can, however, position ourselves for one. As long as we stay in the depths of the cave listening to our fear or anger-filled mental recording, God's presence will simply pass us by. Turn down the white noise and turn up the God volume. God is calling you to reposition yourself to the entrance of your cave with ears open to hear His voice and a face turned toward His presence.

CHAPTER 7

REENVISION YOUR LIFE STORY

One day I received a phone call from a representative of a local university. I had been recommended to offer the invocation at their graduation ceremony. I felt honored that I was being asked to participate in this internationally attended ceremony at the prestigious Rockefeller Chapel on the campus of University of Chicago.

The call came about two years into my ministry. I was starting to struggle with my life "storyboard." In the film industry a storyboard is a sequence of drawings that lays out the narrative flow of a movie. Before the movie is ever produced, the storyboard gives the director a visual picture of where it is going. I was wrestling to make sense of my own storyboard at the time. While my college friends were leaving Chicago to travel to exciting ministries in exotic places, I was staying put. The church was growing and people were being changed, but we were still small and struggling. I was starting my ministry in a neighborhood that most people were trying to leave. The people we were reaching in those days were mainly addicts, felons, and the marginalized. I was wrestling to make ends meet financially and my young wife had to work a full-time job just to keep us afloat. I shopped at thrift stores, fixed my car on the street, found furniture in alleyways, had no insurance, and had ongoing altercations with neighborhood gangbangers. For the first three months of my marriage my wife and I slept on the floor because we could not afford a bed. I never heard her complain—not once—but the pressure of finances and stress of city ministry was tough. Throughout my university days I was convinced I would move back to Europe after college. Nevertheless, through a series of circumstances I can only describe as the hand of God, I found myself the pastor of a struggling church in Chicago. I agreed to serve this congregation for three years until they could find a permanent pastor.

When I arrived at the Rockefeller Chapel, I looked up at the magnificent structure, the tallest building on the University of Chicago campus. The façade was decorated with more than one hundred stone sculptures, representing philosophy and the humanities, religion and university life. I was greeted cordially by the event coordinator who quickly told me what an important event this was. He reminded me that people had traveled from around the world to attend this ceremony. They had an impressive list of distinguished guests participating in the event. We went into the green room where I met the college president and other faculty. I put on a long black robe and we briskly made our way up the side aisle to the platform. On our way the coordinator reminded me that this was a nonsectarian event and there would be people from many religious backgrounds at this gathering. He said I had the reputation of being an intelligent young pastor so he knew I would understand if he asked me not to be sectarian in my comments. When I asked what exactly he meant, he said I should keep my prayers generic so as not to offend anyone in attendance. Reference to Jesus Christ would make people feel uncomfortable so words like "God" or "Supreme Being" would be more appropriate in this setting. Before I could respond, we were ushered onto the stage.

I sat on the platform facing the international crowd. I could see that there were many ethnicities represented. I glanced at the stately elegance of this historical chapel and thought, *What a contrast to the little church I preach in on Sundays!* This chapel was filled with the elite of society. I spent my days working with felons and addicts.

I snapped out of my thoughts when I heard the master of ceremony announce, "And now we have Reverend Jobe, who will lead us in an invocation to start today's ceremony."

HE SAID I SHOULD keep my prayers generic so as not to offend anyone in attendance.

I stepped to the podium, cleared my throat, looked out at the crowd, and prayed a generic, bland, nonsectarian prayer. The event coordinator nodded approvingly as I walked back to my seat. As soon as I sat down I felt a wave of conviction flood my spirit. What flashed through my mind were Paul's words: "For I am not ashamed of the gospel, because it is the power of God that brings salvation to everyone who believes: first to the Jew, then to the Gentile" (Romans 1:16).

I had started living with a storyboard in which I saw myself as a poor, forgotten inner-city pastor who would spend his years struggling in obscurity. That storyboard drove me to seek acceptance at the expense of my core values.

That day on the prestigious Rockefeller Chapel platform I repented before God. I was oblivious to what any speaker said behind the podium that morning. I was preoccupied with an intense internal conversation. Then I heard a voice say, "And now Reverend Jobe will bring our time to an end with a closing benediction."

I practically jumped to my feet. As I approached the podium I saw a different picture. Instead of a poor, forgotten little pastor stuck in life, I saw a picture of a bold servant of God not bending to the pressure of denying the name of Jesus. I stood up with new courage and fresh confidence. I said, "I know this is a nonsectarian event. My intention is not to offend anyone. But I will pray in the only name I know how to pray, the name of Jesus." This time I prayed with authority and assurance in the name of Jesus Christ. When I finished praying I did not wait to get a nod from the event coordinator. I quickly made my way down the aisle with my robes swishing behind me.

Halfway down the aisle a young woman stepped out in front of me. "Reverend Jobe," she said.

"Yes?" I braced myself for a verbal assault.

"Thank you," she said. "I have been at several graduation ceremonies and never once has the pastor had the courage to pray in Jesus' name. Thank you for your courage."

That day I learned an important lesson. I realized how easily my warped mental storyboard affects how I see myself and how I behave under pressure. I determined before God that day that I would never allow the pressure of society to silence the power of His name from my lips.

WHAT'S ON YOUR STORYBOARD?

Our perception of reality affects the way we live and act. Often the mental picture we carry to define our reality does not match God's picture. Only when we discover the story-board that is defining our life and align it with God's story-board can we begin to live on target with the mission of God.

Elijah had drawn a mental picture of himself and his life story. In this storyboard every person in Israel had turned their backs on God and he was the only solitary faithful believer standing strong. He was convinced he stood with the world against him.

Dealing with distorted thinking is not simply a matter of rebooting our thinking, as we saw in the previous chapter. It's also a matter of reenvisioning our personal storyboard from God's perspective. That means we have to erase and repaint as God directs us.

Notice how God masterfully begins to paint a whole new image in contrast to the image Elijah presented:

The Lord said to him, "Go back the way you came, and go to the Desert of Damascus. When you get there, anoint Hazael king over Aram. Also, anoint Jehu son of Nimshi king over Israel, and anoint Elisha son of Shaphat from Abel Meholah to succeed you as prophet. Jehu will put to death any who escape the sword of Hazael, and Elisha will put to death any who escape the sword of Jehu. Yet I reserve seven thousand in Israel—all whose knees have not bowed down to Baal and whose mouths have not kissed him." (1 Kings 19:15–18)

In His response to Elijah, God addresses each distorted image Elijah has presented and carefully redrafts his storyboard.

Elijah: "I have done my part, but nothing is working out."

God: "Go back the way you came. You can face your problems."

Elijah: "I have reached out to people. They are all against me."

God: "There are seven thousand who have not bowed their knee."

Elijah: "I am all alone. No one is on my side."

God: "I have appointed you partners and a successor."

Elijah: "I have a dark future. Everyone is out to destroy me."

God: "You will succeed at overcoming all your enemies."

The prophet Elijah is not the only person that has struggled with a distorted storyboard. The man referred to as the "father of faith" battled to keep his picture clear and focused.

REFRESH YOUR STORYBOARD

Abraham is a prime example of the power of living by a divine picture. Abraham and Sarah, his wife, were childless. God promised Abraham that one day he would be the father of a great nation. As the years passed, Abraham struggled to maintain his faith and cling to the promise God had given him. Since Abraham remained childless, he offered to fulfill this promise through his servant Eliezer of Damascus. God responded to Abraham emphatically, "This man will not be your heir; but one who will come forth from your own body, he shall be your heir" (Genesis 15:4 NASB).

To strengthen Abraham's faith God gave him a new mental picture. He took Abraham out on a clear Middle Eastern night and invited Abraham to look to the stars, and said, "Now look toward the heavens, and count the stars, if you are able to count them." God added, "So shall your descendants be" (Genesis 15:5 NASB).

To strengthen Abraham's faith, God had to give him a fresh mental picture, a new storyboard. From that moment on Abraham revisited the picture of a sky filled with stars to strengthen his faith. I can imagine that in moments of discouragement Abraham closed his eyes and remembered the sight of thousands of stars, and the voice of God saying, "So shall your descendants be." When he saw fathers taking a stroll with their children, he remembered the stars. When young mothers proudly introduced their new baby boys, he remembered the stars. When his wife Sarah cried herself to sleep, longing for a family, he remembered the stars. When he looked at his one-hundred-year-old wrinkled face in the mirror he remembered the stars. When doubt and discouragement dragged down his faith, he must have waited until dark and stepped out of his tent to gaze once again at the stars. As he looked at the stars that filled the sky his spirits lifted as he pictured the faces of his children and grandchildren emerging from each star.

This new, clear image was Abraham's defining storyboard. Much of what the Scriptures seek to do is to erase misleading images built on faulty distortions and repaint new images based on God's truth and perspective.

FRESH ENCOUNTERS

The prophet Elijah was driven to his dark cave by the distorted image that he kept seeing over and over in his head. Not until Elijah had a fresh encounter with God's presence was he able to hear the divine word that painted a new picture of his life and destiny.

In January 1964, my parents, Bob and Minnie Jobe, stepped aboard an airplane that carried them to a lifetime of adventure on foreign soils. Costa Rica, Chile, and Spain were their home for the next forty years. They boarded that plane with their two boys Bob Jr. (two years old) and me (six months). My sister, Marsela, was born three years later in a hospital on the coast of Chile.

After a year of learning the language in San Jose, Costa Rica, our family headed for Viña del Mar, near Valparaiso, Chile. There my parents threw themselves into rugged church planting. I can still clearly picture Trompo, the horse Dad would ride to remote villages in the hills of Chile to lead Bible studies with people in rural towns. As a boy I heard the stories of people's conversions, Bible studies in dirt-floor huts, and confrontations with angry village witch doctors as he traveled on horseback to remote areas.

In 1971 our family arrived in Spain, our new mission field. Chile had been a good experience, but my parents' hearts had become burdened by what some called the "last frontier" of the Spanish-speaking world. They wanted to go to the unreached places. After "spying out the land," my parents discovered that there were still two cities in Spain with over 100,000 people and no evangelical church. They moved to a small town three miles outside their target city, Burgos.

Years later I discovered that George Verwer (founder of Operation Mobilization) and a couple of his buddies had been through Burgos in 1970. They had been burdened to find a city of that size with no gospel-preaching church and had prayed fervently that God would raise a work in that city in northern Spain. One year later my parents arrived with a team of people to start a church.

I CAN IMAGINE that in moments of discouragement Abraham closed his eyes and remembered the sight of thousands of stars.

For the first five years this small band of believers met in an old whitewashed horse stable on the edge of town. Our "sanctuary" was rough to say the least, with rustic wooden beams, the horse troughs, and the occasional mouse during the worship service. The villagers viewed outsiders with great suspicion. The old town priest publicly denounced us and prohibited the local children from having contact with the *Americanos*. My father was interrogated by the secret police on numerous occasions. People were afraid to come to our meetings or be seen speaking to us publicly. A couple of times people met with my father in secret to discuss spiritual matters, but the team made little progress.

Desperate for a breakthrough, my father and two other missionaries vowed to pray together on a hill overlooking the village until God made a way. Several mornings a week they cried out for the city of Burgos and the small town of Quintanadueñas. Morning after morning they woke up early and drove to that prayer spot to cry out for the people of Burgos. They had to fight the dark mental picture that kept surfacing, the picture of a city too difficult to reach. They battled the image of missionaries returning home discouraged and defeated with no fruit to show for their efforts. Those early morning prayer meetings began with heavy burdens and desperate cries for a move of God.

As they continued to cry out, their heavy prayers began to give way to glimpses of hope and renewed faith. The presence of God met them in a fresh new way. They began to pray with greater expectation and new anticipation. They began to see the city with fresh new eyes. They prayed in faith for a city that would be known throughout Spain for the move of God. A city that would see hundreds of young people come to Christ and see them live radically for Jesus. Nothing in the physical realm had changed but something in the spiritual atmosphere seemed different. Within a short time, dozens of young people hungry for God began showing up at the horse-stable church. Authentic conversions were accompanied by radical testimonies. Soon that whitewashed horse stable was packed with teenagers hungry for God. Within a couple of years hundreds of young people came to Christ in a dramatic renewal movement that had long-term repercussions on many parts of

THEY HAD TO FIGHT the dark mental picture that kept surfacing, the picture of a city too difficult to reach.

Spain. The city of Burgos came to be known as a place where God was moving in an extraordinary way.

Recently I visited my childhood village. The whitewashed stable has been renovated into a Christian drug rehabilitation center. Many Christians live in that town now, and a Christian church is under construction on the edge of town.

Never is our storyboard as clear as it is in the light of a fresh God encounter. My father and his team saw in faith a harvest of changed lives before it ever happened.

POCKET-SIZE GODS

One of the great challenges for every generation of God followers is not allowing the image of God to be reshaped and downsized by their contemporary culture. In Elijah's day, Israel's problem was not that they rejected God altogether but that they added Him to their assortment of gods. Israel had been a nomadic shepherding people, so when they finally settled in their land and began farming, they discovered that people in that region worshiped gods of fertility and harvest. The new Israelite farmers adapted the ways of the farmers of that region. They still believed in the God of Abraham, Isaac, and Jacob, but they added Baal and Ashterah to the religious menu. Theologians call this practice syncretism. What Israel needed was to see God for who He was.

Over a century later another prophet named Isaiah faced the same challenge. Isaiah chapter 6 describes an experience that exposed Isaiah afresh to the untarnished image of God that turned his world upside down and launched him to a renewed calling. It happened in the "year that King Uzziah died." King Uzziah was king of Judah and had started his rule when he was only sixteen years old, the age of a sophomore in high school. Uzziah had been coached by Zechariah, a godly mentor, and for the first part of his reign he did well.

The change was gradual: "But after Uzziah became powerful, his pride led to his downfall" (2 Chronicles 26:16). As Uzziah gained experience, his reverence for God diminished. The tragic climax came when Uzziah's arrogance drove him to ignore God's law and decide that he would burn incense on the altar. Only the priests set apart unto God were permitted to perform this duty. Uzziah understood that. But he boldly defied the high priest and disregarded his attempts to stop him.

Uzziah's attitude trickled down to the people. The people of Judah continued corrupt practices, including worshiping idols of the gods of neighboring nations. The spiritual environment of Isaiah's time was one of moral and spiritual decay. People had become rebellious and hardened their hearts toward God.

Isaiah lived in a God-shrinking culture much like our culture today. God was being reduced to a pocket-size rabbit's foot to help people in time of need. Pocket-size gods don't demand our respect or reverence. Pocket-size gods revolve around our needs and can be used at our convenience. Pocket-size gods ruin vision and water down the passion of people with a calling on their life.

I like the way Francis Chan describes this general attitude in his book *Crazy Love*.

The core problem isn't the fact that we're lukewarm, halfhearted, or stagnant Christians. The crux of it all is why we are this way, and it is because we have an inaccurate view of God. We see Him as a benevolent Being who is satisfied when people manage to fit Him into their lives in some small way. We forget that God never had an identity crisis. He knows that He's great and deserves to be the center of our lives.[1]

Isaiah was at the temple one day, when he was exposed to a fresh vision of God. In his own words he said:

I saw the Lord, high and exalted, seated on a throne; and the train of his robe filled the temple. Above him were seraphim, each with six wings: With two wings they covered their faces, with two they covered their feet, and with two they were flying. And they were calling to one another: "Holy, holy, holy is the Lord Almighty; the whole earth is full of his glory." At the sound of their voices the doorposts and thresholds shook and the temple was filled with smoke. (Isaiah 6:1–4)

This means that the One who is holy is uniquely holy, with no rivals or competition. Exposure to God's presence will stir within us a new awareness of who we are and what we need to do. "Woe to me!" Isaiah cried in response. "I am ruined! For I am a man of unclean lips, and I live among a people of unclean lips, and my eyes have seen the King, the Lord Almighty" (Isaiah 6:5). The more clearly Isaiah saw God, the more aware Isaiah became of his own inadequacy.

The very altar Uzziah desecrated fifteen years earlier because of his small view of God was now being used to touch and purify Isaiah. When Isaiah's lips were touched by the burning coal, God declared him holy. The painful cleansing process was necessary before Isaiah could fulfill the task to which God was calling him.

Isaiah's fresh encounter with God's powerful presence gave him a new urgency to pursue his call. His clear sense of calling came on the heels of a fresh encounter with the magnitude of God. Isaiah heard the Lord saying, "Whom shall I send? And who will go for us?" [And he rose to the call.] "Here am I. Send me!" (Isaiah 6:8).

William Booth, the fiery founder of the Salvation Army, scoffed at those who did not consider themselves called by God. " 'Not *called*,' did you say?" he exclaimed. "'Not *heard* the call,' I think you should say." He continued:

> Put your ear down to the Bible, and hear him bid you
> go and pull poor sinners out of the fire of sin. Put your
> ear down to the burdened, agonized heart of human-
> ity, and listen to its pitying wail for help. Go and stand
> by the gates of Hell, and hear the damned entreat you
> to go to their father's house, and bid their brothers,
> and sisters, and servants, and masters not to come
> there. And then look the Christ in the face, whose
> mercy you profess to have got, and whose words you
> have promised to obey, and tell Him whether you will
> join us heart and soul and body and circumstances in
> the march to publish his mercy to all the world.[2]

Our life and call come into perspective when we catch a
clear vision of God and His mission.

ON THE BEACH

My first semester at college was difficult. I wrestled with
what I wanted to do with my life and future. I had a part-time
job working for a doctor who owned a boating magazine and
lived in an exclusive neighborhood in downtown Chicago.
After numerous conversations with my boss I began to doubt
whether I should come back to Bible college the next semester.
I had no idea what I would do after my schooling and I began
to feel like I should have a "real degree" to survive in the "real
world." The doctor, who was not a Christian, questioned why I

was wasting a sharp mind just studying the Bible and theology. He reasoned, "You can have your faith, but you need a career to make a living." When the semester ended, I was hired for a summer job at a hotel in a coastal town in southern France.

Someone had given me a copy of A. W. Tozer's *Knowledge of the Holy*. After work I would jog down to the oceanfront, take a swim, and read from the book. It wasn't the ideal place to read *Knowledge of the Holy* since beaches in southern France are not known for their modesty. But that summer I realized that the pathway to understanding my purpose started with understanding my Creator. Tozer put it this way:

> What comes into our minds when we think about God is the most important thing about us. The history of mankind will probably show that no people has ever risen above its religion, and man's spiritual history will positively demonstrate that no religion has ever been greater than its idea of God. Worship is pure or base as the worshiper entertains high or low thoughts of God.[3]

I needed to see my storyboard clearly in the light of a fresh divine encounter. My thought pattern that had become distorted by my own insecurities and influenced by a materialistic doctor needed to be exposed to the knowledge of God. That summer was a turning point. I had to answer the question: "What are you doing here, Mark?" For most of the summer I wrestled to answer that question. In the end I had to admit that I had allowed doubt-filled thinking to replace my confidence in God.

In chapter 1 I referred to a woman who stepped into my office and said, "I'm stuck. I feel like a bruised and battered, broken wife." Her marriage had not gone as smoothly as she had hoped. She had lost trust in her husband. Her once gleaming view of their future appeared dark and unclear. She repeated, "I can't get this image out of my mind. I don't feel like that radiant hope-filled bride that I was a year ago." She admitted that she was battling depression and had little hope for their future.

I NEEDED TO SEE my storyboard clearly in the light of a fresh divine encounter.

As I listened to this young bride with her husband sitting beside her I was reminded of the power of pictures. I walked over to my office wall and said, "Imagine this is the picture of the bruised, battered, and broken-down bride that you have spoken of." I took my hand and applied an invisible eraser to the image with a few swipes of my hand. I said, "Let's repaint this picture from God's perspective. You have been hurt and disappointed by your husband but you have not walked out on him. That is not weakness—that is strength." I continued, "You are battling to forgive and trust again. That is not weakness, that is strength." I asked her to look at that wall again and help me paint a new picture. The picture I asked her to see with me was of a brave, valiant warrior bride fighting for the destiny of her marriage and family; a woman of virtue with a radiant face looking toward the future, fighting for what she knows is her God-given destiny.

Over the following weeks she went back over and over to

that new image to remind her of her identity. A few weeks later, her countenance had changed. Her confidence and radiance were back. She was living her new image.

The longer you live with the wrong storyboard the harder it is to erase. That is why men or women who have been abused in childhood have such a hard time erasing distorted images of themselves and their world. They have lived with a lie-based image so long that it warps their identity and worldview. I have had countless conversations with women who struggle with understanding the love of their heavenly Father because of their dysfunctional relationship with their abusive earthly father.

Scripture tells us that the key to transformation is the renewing of our mind. "Do not conform to the pattern of this world, but be transformed by the renewing of your mind. Then you will be able to test and approve what God's will is— his good, pleasing and perfect will" (Romans 12:2). Our storyboard will always be misrepresented until we properly see God in the bigger picture of our board.

What storyboard are you currently living with? Is it a mental picture that contradicts the picture that God has declared over you? Take a moment to visually erase the image that is defining your life. Now allow God to redraw a new mental picture. Let the Master artist craft His image for you and your life. Can you see it begin to emerge? It is carefully and painstakingly painted with you in mind. The sovereign God of the universe is imbedding in your spirit His divine portrait. You have a purpose and a God-given destiny. Prepare to live in this new storyboard.

CHAPTER 8

WALK TOWARD YOUR UNFINISHED BUSINESS

"I have been stuck for several years," Tom said. His voice was shaking. "I don't know how to move forward. I feel like I've been dragging my feet through a long dry desert, but this desert has no end." When Tom became a Christian he was zealous and hungry for God. He grew rapidly and in a few years he was leading the youth group, occasionally preaching on Sunday morning, becoming a key leader in his church. Today, though, his countenance was sad. "Then something happened."

Tom described how in a moment of weakness he was approached by a prostitute and had a sexual encounter with her. With tears streaming down his face he said, "That was seven years ago. I have confessed it to God and begged for His forgiveness, but I feel like I have committed the unpardonable sin, because I still feel stuck. Why am I unable to move forward?"

I stopped him. "Tom, I think you know what you need to do but you have been avoiding the final step."

He stared into my eyes and said, "Oh no. I know where you are going with this. I could never tell my wife. It would devastate her." He paused to regain his composure. "She doesn't deserve this. I can't bear putting her through the pain."

"You're right. She doesn't deserve this," I answered. "But she doesn't deserve to live with a husband who is joyless and spiritually apathetic either. She does deserve the truth and a full confession. She deserves the chance to get her man-of-God husband back."

Tom admitted that he knew years ago that he should bring his issue to the light but because of the pain and shame he had been unwilling. His secret and unwillingness to deal with the hard issues had led him to seven years of stuck living. We prayed together and he vowed he would come clean with his wife when he saw her next. A week later I received an email. It said:

Dear Mark, I have not felt this free and at peace in years. I fully confessed to my wife. It was the hardest thing I have ever done in my life. But I kept remembering your words that my wife deserves something better than a halfhearted spiritually stuck man. For now I am sleeping on the living room couch, but thanking God that I have stepped out of my long desert.

I am happy to report that Tom and his wife are doing great and fully engaged in living for God with a great marriage. Before he could move forward in freedom, Tom had to decide to go to the hard places and deal with the painful issues he was avoiding.

The first question God asked Elijah in his cave experience was, "What are you doing here?" And the first major action step God called Elijah to take was, "Go back the way you came." The most important directive God gave Elijah was to march straight back to the place he was running from. Some people are waiting in the cave for their circumstances to change before they think about stepping out. They believe they are trapped until something beyond their control changes. A fresh encounter with God doesn't change our circumstances but it changes us to face our circumstances.

"The Lord said to him, 'Go back the way you came, and go to the Desert of Damascus'" (1 Kings 19:15).

Do you remember what happened in the Desert of Damascus? This is the place where Elijah, on his way to the cave, spiraled into his suicidal, pity-induced depression. The Desert of Damascus represented the worst point of Elijah's life. It was his lowest moment and most desperate hour. Beyond the desert was Jezebel, the woman who had triggered his run to the cave in the first place. God sent Elijah back to the very same difficult circumstances from which he had run.

Recently a friend who was pregnant told me that she is not going back to the hospital where she had her first baby. When I asked why she said the hospital and staff were great, but she had such a bad labor experience and painful recovery that just walking into that hospital depressed her. I'm sure the thought of the Damascus Desert sent similar feelings through Elijah.

Not only did God send Elijah right back to the place of his worst nightmare but He told him to "anoint Jehu son of Nimshi king over Israel, and anoint Elisha son of Shaphat from Abel Meholah to succeed you as prophet" (1 Kings 19:16). In essence God asked Elijah to set in motion a political coup that would topple his archenemy Jezebel and her reign of terror. Not only did God direct Elijah to go back to his problem. He also asked him to tackle his major fear head-on.

Issue avoidance has become a national pastime. If it is difficult, painful, or demanding, we avoid it as long as we can. Countless couples avoid dealing with the root issues of their marriage problems and end up in divorce court. Governments avoid dealing with real issues of debt until it becomes an economic crisis. Millions of Americans avoid dealing with the issues that lead to addictions until they need to go to rehab. Elijah was tired of dealing with the stress and tension of his calling and hit a tipping point where he just ran. He reached a point of exhaustion and told himself, "All this work and sacrifice has not made a difference, and I will end up one more dead prophet." He became gripped with the fear of failure. Instead of facing his issues he ran and hid. He sat down under a broom tree and prayed, "I have had enough, Lord . . . Take my life; I am no better than my ancestors" (1 Kings 19:4).

A fresh encounter with God spun Elijah around. His back had been toward his problem but his encounter with the presence of God sent him headfirst toward his unresolved issue.

NEW SEASONS AND
UNFINISHED BUSINESS

Most people want relief from a situation that does not involve facing their issues and dealing with their problems. The resentful husband doesn't want marriage counseling; he wants to find a new wife. The disgruntled church member doesn't want to work through her conflict with the usher; she wants to find a new church. The indebted young man doesn't want to work with a financial counselor; he would rather just play the lottery. The single woman doesn't want to deal with what drives her from one bad relationship to another; she just wants to join a new dating service. The compulsive eater doesn't want to deal with what compels her to binge; she just wants a new diet pill.

ISSUE AVOIDANCE has become a national pastime.

We get stuck in life when we avoid the pain of dealing with our issues. Issue avoidance postpones the immediate pain but increases the long-term consequences and compounds the problems. Our journey to a new season involves dealing with the issues we have been avoiding. It demands that we go to the hard places before we can move on. God's challenge to Elijah to "go back the way you came" meant that Elijah had to return to confront the very fear and disillusionment he was running from. He had to travel back through the valley of depression and come face-to-face with his greatest fear. The only way forward is going back and confronting our sticking points.

Life consists of a continual series of transitions from one season to the next. Every new season is marked by borders that we must cross without getting stuck. I have discovered that un-dealt-with issues surface most during times of transition.

The first couple I ever married was an introduction to this principle. I had been visiting George and Marcy regularly. Finally George, an ex-addict, decided he wanted to give his life to Christ and Marcy soon followed. They had been living together for close to ten years already and had a seven-year-old son. I asked George to "couch it" until they got married. It was hard for George to understand why, after ten years and one kid, that God wouldn't understand them sleeping together. But finally they both agreed. We planned a small, quick wedding. About two days before the wedding Marcy took me aside and wanted to talk. She explained that about four years earlier she and George had separated for a few months. She was in desperate need of cash for her own apartment. To pay her bills she had married an undocumented immigrant who paid her $5,000 cash in an effort to become legal. She had not been physically involved and she had never seen him again after the civil ceremony. Marcy felt guilty about the pseudomarriage and wanted to confess it to me before the wedding. I explained that polygamy was illegal in the state of Illinois and I could not marry her until we worked through this issue.

Unfortunately, we had to contact all the invited guests a couple of days before the wedding and postpone the marriage for "personal reasons." I had to sit through a tough conversation with her and George, who knew nothing about the fake marriage. It took us about three months to sort through a "divorce" and finally marry George and Marcy. They left on their honeymoon, and Dee and I watched their son.

Marcy's unresolved issue was not a big deal until she was ready to move to a new season. Then it became a major sticking point that kept her from moving to her new season. She was moving out of singleness to a new season of marriage to the man that she loved, but she was stopped in her tracks by an unresolved issue. There was no way around it. Either she stayed in the old season of singleness or confronted her past failure to move forward in marriage.

Someone once said that the only thing consistent in life is that it is always changing. I heard of an interview with a man who had turned a hundred years old. The reporter mused, "You must have seen a lot of changes during the last century."

"Yes I have," said the centenarian, "and I've been against every single one of them."

Some of us go through life with that same mentality. We resist every new season that comes our way. We spend a lot of time stuck at the border of new seasons refusing to step across the line until we are forced to.

A few years ago my mother called and informed me that my father had suddenly become very sick. I called my brother, Bob, and we both scrambled to organize an emergency trip to Spain where my father lived. When we arrived at O'Hare I showed the TSA agent my passport, only to discover it was expired. I had been living with an expired passport for a few months but it wasn't an issue until I tried to cross the US border. My stomach sank as I waved goodbye to my brother

SOME OF US RESIST every new season that comes our way.

who boarded the plane without me.

I got in my car and drove straight to the federal building in downtown Chicago where I had previously renewed my passport. When I tried to enter the building I was stopped by security. With some exasperation I explained I needed to renew my passport immediately for a family emergency. The security guard said, "I'm sorry, sir, but the federal government is closed until they can agree on a budget."

Incredulous, I asked, "Well, how long is that going to take?"

He shrugged and said, "No one knows, but we all hope it will be soon." Here I was, stuck in Chicago with a father seriously ill in a hospital bed in Spain. My passport was expired and the federal government was closed. After numerous calls I finally got hold of someone who could answer my questions. They informed me that I would not be able to renew my passport until the federal government reopened. I pressed for an emergency passport and was told that the only emergency passports that they were granting were in case of death. They would renew a passport if I proved that I was picking up the body of an immediate family member but not for illnesses. I hung up the phone frustrated and discouraged. I prayed, "Lord, my father needs me now. They are telling me it is impossible to get to Spain, but I know You are the great door opener. Make a way, Lord." I picked up the phone and made one last desperate phone call to Washington to the department head who had the power to grant exceptions. I hung up thinking that I would have to resign myself to waiting.

I received a phone call thirty minutes later saying, "Mr. Jobe, we have granted your request. Go to the federal building and we will open up the office for you to renew your passport." I drove downtown as quickly as possible. When I walked in that building the security guard said, "Young man, you must have some very high connections for them to open this office just for you." I looked at him with confidence and boldly said, "You can't even imagine how high my connections go!" With my passport in hand I went right across the border and made it to my father's bedside in northern Spain the next day. Five days later he passed away. I will forever be grateful for the few days I was able to spend with my father before his home going. My expired passport almost made me miss out on the last days of my father's life.

I learned a valuable lesson that day. Unfinished business will stop us from crossing borders at key times in our life. On the way across the border our un-dealt-with issues become major sticking points that can cause us to miss out on key opportunities in life.

THE PROBLEM WITH
UNFINISHED BUSINESS

Exodus 4:18–31 recounts a very unusual story. The setting could be taken straight from an Alfred Hitchcock horror flick. There's a cheap motel, a man gasping for breath, a child lying, groaning, in a puddle of blood, a half-crazed woman with a sharp bloody object in her hand, and a piece of human flesh lying on the floor. This obscure passage in Exodus exposes the danger of trying to cross borders with unfinished business.

"At a lodging place on the way, the Lord met Moses and was about to kill him. But Zipporah took a flint knife, cut off her son's foreskin and touched Moses' feet with it" (Exodus 4:24–25).

Moses had been reawakened by the call at the burning bush. He had been reluctant, insecure, and unconvinced, but with some divine prodding, Moses said yes to God. After a forty-year detour Moses was finally back on mission to fulfill his life's call and liberate the people of Israel from four hundred years of slavery. He packed up his bags, said goodbye to his father-in-law, Jethro, and set out on his journey back to Egypt with his wife, Zipporah, and his two young sons. He stopped at a lodge on the way and something extraordinary happened. God tried to kill him. You read that correctly. Scripture tells us that "the Lord met Moses and was about to kill him." Why on earth would God call Moses and then try to kill him? After all, Moses was on a mission responding in obedience to the call of God.

Moses had unfinished business that surfaced as he tried to cross the spiritual border into his calling. When he was taking care of sheep in his shepherd season it didn't seem to be an issue, but the passport control is alerted when he is about to cross this significant spiritual border in his life.

Moses was well aware that part of embracing his Jewish roots was to submit to the practice of circumcising all male children. Maybe he viewed it as a barbaric practice since he was raised in the sophistication of an Egyptian culture. Perhaps

Zipporah, his wife, objected to the rite of circumcision since she was not an Israelite and may have thought it a strange custom. Maybe they had postponed it because the time never seemed right and it fell low on the priority list. Whatever the reason, Moses had postponed obeying, and now as he moved to his higher calling it had become a major roadblock.

I have discovered that if we avoid dealing with important issues they will most certainly surface later at very inconvenient times. By the time the circumcision of his eldest son became a priority for Moses, it was a matter of life and death. This new season Moses was entering brought with it higher expectations of holiness. It was time for him to lay aside his compromise and cross the border into a new season.

But because Moses had delayed his obedience, Zipporah ended up doing the difficult work that her husband, Moses, should have done years before. And she resented it. When someone else has to do your dirty work because you dropped the ball, they will not be happy. Moses was virtually on his deathbed and Zipporah sprang into action. She quickly grabbed a sharp rock and, with determination and disgust, she circumcised her screaming son to save the life of her husband.

I can picture her son at the age of twenty-five in a therapy support group discussing the trauma of that night. "Hi my name is Gershom. I remember that night as if it were yesterday. My mother came after me with a sharp rock. I had no idea why she was doing it. I remember the screaming, the blood, the pain, and the confusion." The people around him gasp in horror at his traumatic childhood and shake their heads in disbelief at his dysfunctional family.

When we postpone obedience because it seems uncomfortable, we are only postponing the pain and increasing the problem. Eventually all our unfinished business will surface.

THE SIN BIN

I had only been a pastor for two years and the little church on 44th and Paulina was continuing to grow with mostly non-churched people. This made for a very exciting atmosphere but also a very messy one. During one season God began to deal with us about the need to clean house and walk in purity before Him. Many of the young converts had been immersed in superstitions, idolatry, and addictions. A large number of our new church members came from wild lifestyles filled with destructive habits and immorality. To visually emphasize the challenge of "cleaning house," I placed a large black barrel in the entrance to our building and labeled it the "Sin Bin." The idea was that people would go through their house and rid themselves of things that represented practices of their old life that were not pleasing to God. The barrel quickly filled with items.

One lady brought a bag of small statues that she and her relatives had prayed to and venerated as sacred. She came to me and said, "Pastor, I'm cleaning house and need to get rid of these statues." She paused. "Could you please dispose of them for me." Her son later confided that although she was convicted by the Word, she was afraid of destroying the statues herself because of the possible retaliation that might come upon her. She figured she would let me destroy them and see if I came down with some strange disease or twitch in the eye induced by her sacred statues. I had a little private idol-smashing party with my hammer in the back alley behind my house.

People were responding to the challenge with repentance and conviction. One Sunday evening at the end of a service a newcomer came to the front of the church for prayer. He reached in his pocket and with tears in his eyes laid a bag of cocaine on the altar. I was a little nervous about giving the bag to the ushers since most of them were recent ex-addicts. We decided that the toilet was a better option for the drugs than the Sin Bin, so as not to add extra temptation.

A few days later I received a phone call from a brother named Tony, who sounded a little nervous. He said, "Pastor, I have something for the Sin Bin that I want to get rid of."

"Can you wait until Sunday?" I asked.

"No," he said. "I need to get rid of it tonight!" He came to my house with two bags in his hand. He explained that he was having a Bible study with someone that had just started visiting the church a few weeks earlier. The man had broken under conviction and handed him two stacks of magazines full of underage pornography. Tony explained that he did not want that filth in his house so he figured I would know what to do with it. My wife was livid he had brought the porn magazines to our house. We kept the bags on the back porch until the next day. In the morning I drove to the church with the two bags of porn in

HE REACHED IN HIS pocket and with tears in his eyes laid a bag of cocaine on the altar.

my backseat. I drove very slowly and prayed all the way that I would not get into a car accident. I could just imagine the headlines, "Pastor in car accident found with a stack of pornography." I put the stack of magazines at the bottom of the Sin Bin.

By this time the bin was overflowing with music tapes, *Playboy* magazines, religious artifacts, cultish items, and drug paraphernalia. Someone had even placed their small TV in the bin. I decided we should have a bonfire ceremony like Paul had done in Ephesus when they burned a pile of pagan witchcraft accessories. So during a Sunday evening service we all marched down the front stairs to the small yard in front of the church. We secured an extra large double size barrel grill, dumped all the Sin Bin content on the oversized grill and doused it with lighter fluid as we sang songs of worship with our guitars.

Everything seemed to be going well at first. People were singing passionately and the symbolic act was truly moving. What I did not expect is how high the flames would get and how black the cloud of smoke would be that billowed from that pile. Within moments dozens of neighbors were on their front porch to see the fire at the corner church. A crowd was gathering and the smoke was getting worse. One neighbor yelled, "What are you people trying to do, burn the neighborhood down?" Then above the singing and neighborhood voices, to my dismay, I heard the familiar siren of a fire truck moving quickly toward us. The truck pulled up within feet of the worshiping crowd and several adrenaline-stoked firefighters jumped off the truck, somewhat confused as to what was happening. Fortunately, Nick Bailey, a seasoned fireman from our church, pulled the captain aside and tried to convince him that this was a legitimate religious ceremony. The captain responded in no uncertain terms that religious ceremony or not, the fire needed to be put out immediately. They helped us put out the fire, and we ended the bonfire with great rejoicing and celebrating the freedom that Jesus brings.

Though I would not recommend a Sin Bin bonfire in the city of Chicago, I do believe that dealing with our issues is vital. Nothing can sabotage the power of the presence of God in an individual or congregation like the lingering issues that need to be dealt with. Anyone who gets serious about welcoming the presence of God will have a renewed passion for obedience and a clean slate.

Delayed obedience is another form of disobedience. Stepping boldly into your unresolved issues is key to breaking out of your cave. Elijah could not move into his next season without directly confronting the fears that had driven his run to the cave.

RENEWAL AND THE HARD PLACES

This same principle not only applies to individual lives but also to marriages, families, churches, communities, companies, and countries.

Over the last decade I have had the incredible opportunity to be a part of restarting nine historic churches in Chicago. Some of these churches were established well over a century ago. By the time they contact us they are usually in pretty bad shape, and their stories are usually quite similar. They were founded by a committed group of pioneers who sacrificed to construct the church building and preach the gospel of Jesus Christ. Often there are decades of growth, healthy impact, missionary activity—the glory days. But inevitably the first generation passes on, neighborhoods change, and the congregation struggles to survive. Often the core that is left in these historic urban temples is faced with difficult decisions. Many of these congregations close and their legacy and sacred space is lost in the hustle of fast-paced urban living. I have found great satisfaction in helping to keep alive the gospel flame in these sacred spaces. Our team has made it part of our mission to restart these struggling churches with dignity and honor. We have learned to celebrate their past as part of our adopted past. To see historic churches filled with life again and regaining their original purpose has been thrilling.

The greatest difference between historic churches that are able to restart and those that die is their willingness to go to the hard places and take the bold steps. Many churches know they are not going to survive but find it too painful to go to the hard places of change. They are more comfortable with an old problem than with a new solution. They would rather die the same than go on living differently.

When I first met the congregation at Galilee Baptist Church, I was convinced that a partnership would be a complete mismatch. They were a historic church with a very traditional culture and a congregation that was predominantly in its seventies and eighties. New Life was a young church with hundreds of newer believers. Galilee's music director led the congregation in worship through historic hymns accompanied by the organ. New Life had a worship band with drums, electric guitars, bass, and percussion. Most of our musicians used to play in bars and rock bands before coming to Christ.

At our first meeting I expressed my reservations about entering a potentially conflictive culture clash. But as I heard the heart of these elderly believers my reluctance began to give way to hope and vision. The defining moment came when I met with Chuck McWherter, a man in his seventies who had been chairman of the board for years. He looked at me and said, "Mark, I have been a part of this church for over forty years. I love these people and this church, but I know we need to change to survive. I am willing to do whatever it takes to continue to reach people for Christ." That was the turning point. After that conversation I knew we had a chance. Chuck assured me he was willing to lead the people to the hard places of change.

We shared a common love for Jesus and a desire to see the gospel change lives. They were frustrated that their beloved church was dwindling and struggling to connect with the community. We were struggling to find strategic ways of bringing the gospel to various communities. We had people and they had a building. They had history and we had energy. We understood the culture of the community and they understood the heritage of their sacred space. They had seasoned veterans of the faith, and we had many young believers looking for examples to inspire them.

Things moved quickly and within about five months of our initial contact we were celebrating a grand opening. Out of the thirty original members about twenty chose to stay. Most of the members who left went to small traditional churches that were just like Galilee had been. Those who stayed fastened their seat belts for a fast ride down the road of change. The original members that remained have been an incredible source of encouragement, stability, faith, and example. Most of them have more ministry opportunities now than they had in years.

The church on the corner of Damen and Wellington once known as Galilee Baptist Church is a hub of ministry activity. New Life West Lake View has a full nursery. People are coming to Christ and the multiple worship services minister to a couple hundred people from the community each week. All because they were willing to go to the hard places to change and refuse to guard a culture of comfort.

Many people continue year after year knowing that they need to change, knowing that they are stuck, but refusing to go to the hard places. Their restart never comes because they avoid the pain of change.

Is there an issue you have been avoiding? Have you been running from a step of obedience you know you need to take? Have you been making excuses about timing and right setting? Are you stuck at the border of a new season unable to cross? What issue do you need to deal with—boldly and head-on—before you move to your new season? It is time to face your toughest issue and walk straight into the hard places. It's time to update your passport and move on.

CHAPTER 9

REDISCOVER YOUR BOUNDARIES

I reluctantly agreed to help coach the first- and second-grade soccer team my son had recently joined. I soon discovered that the best job was that of Assistant Coach. That job allowed me to yell on the sidelines along with the head coach, but not have to deal with weekly calls and administrative busywork. At our first practice I realized that these little players didn't know much about soccer and really just wanted to kick the ball. When our first official soccer game began we looked good. The boys wore their matching uniforms, shin guards, cleated shoes, and numbers on the back of their shirts. We huddled in a circle, put our hands together, and yelled out our team name. The head coach and I positioned the players on the field and reminded them to play hard. When the referee blew the whistle, I watched in dismay as my team quickly abandoned their assigned positions and as a wild horde, chased after the black-and-white soccer ball.

Only our goalie stayed in his position and I could tell he was using all the willpower he could muster not to join the chase. The young players from both teams crowded in a circle, pushing and shoving to try to get their foot on the ball. Periodically a kid would get a good kick and the ball would fly out of the crowded circle. The players would look around and take off running toward the ball again.

At halftime the coach and I gathered the panting, red-faced players and gave them one instruction, "Stay in your position." We assured them that the ball would eventually come to their area, but they needed to play their position. We drew some imaginary boundary circles on the floor and told them, "Play your position and stay in your boundaries." Boundaries, we explained to the kids, meant that each team member needed to play within their lines and pass the ball to another player when they crossed the line. It was a simple system, but it worked. Once these young soccer players learned to play their positions we started winning games. Without boundaries there was chaos as each soccer player tried to play the whole field by themselves. Without boundaries every player acted as a one-man team trying to score goals. As a result they were tired, ineffective, and losing games. When they learned to play their position and stay in their boundaries we started winning. We didn't go on to win the World Cup but we did learn some valuable lessons. The first-grade soccer players struggled to learn the same lesson that Elijah had to wrestle with: how to play his position and remain in bounds. Elijah had been a one-man team, but he ended up red-faced and exhausted. Life without boundaries is ultimately unsustainable and unhealthy.

TAKING ON MORE
THAN GOD GAVE YOU

Elijah ended up in the cave of self-pity and isolation in part because he had taken on more than God had given him. He hadn't learned to play within the boundaries of his calling. Before he exited the cave, God helped him clarify his calling and release control over areas that were not his to manage. Elijah found new release when he delegated areas of responsibility to other people.

God sent Elijah back to his nightmare setting and the job that he had quit. But this time Elijah had a plan that included recruiting a team and releasing responsibility. To put it another way, not only did God give Elijah a plan to break out of isolation, but He also set in motion a plan to limit Elijah's responsibilities and narrow his call: "The Lord said to him, 'Go back the way you came, and go to the Desert of Damascus. When you get there, anoint Hazael king over Aram. Also, anoint Jehu son of Nimshi king over Israel, and anoint Elisha son of Shaphat from Abel Meholah to succeed you as prophet'" (1 Kings 19:15–16).

The first-grade soccer players struggled to learn the same lesson that Elijah had to wrestle with: how to play his position and remain in bounds. Like many of us, Elijah had assumed responsibilities that God had never called him to handle. It took three leaders to successfully manage the job Elijah was trying to accomplish by himself. Elijah exited the cave with clear instructions to delegate responsibility for the political leadership of Syria (Aram) to Hazael and the political leadership of Israel to Nimshi. He was also told to delegate authority to a young leader named Elisha, who would succeed him in the spiritual leadership of Israel.

Knowing what we are *not* called to do is just as important as knowing what we are called to do. The vitality and sustainability of your mission and calling depends on you knowing your limits. Setting down those things that you were never meant to carry frees up energy and resources with which you can address your main calling.

I believe that every person has been created by design with a divine purpose in mind. I love the way the apostle Paul says it in his letter to the Ephesians. "For it is by grace you have been saved," he writes, "through faith—and this is not from yourselves, it is the gift of God—not by works, so that no one can boast. For we are God's handiwork, created in Christ Jesus to do good works, which God prepared in advance for us to do" (Ephesians 2:8–10).

Every Christian is called to a relationship with God through His Son, Jesus Christ. Once we have come to Christ, then we are all called to live on mission with Him. There are not some who are called and some who are not. We are all called. The question is how we respond.

INCREASING BY RELEASING

"I think it's time for me to move on and start something new," I blurted out. Unfortunately for me, the leadership team I had raised up was firm. They did not feel it was the right time for a leadership transition.

The church had grown from fewer than twenty to about

two hundred fifty people, and I was ready to move on. The budget had grown enough to give someone a legitimate salary. We had replaced our a cappella singing with a worship band. Our leadership was functioning with committed volunteer couples. We had outgrown our facility and were renting a grade-school auditorium. The church was chaotically healthy and brimming with new believers. Nevertheless, the thrill of starting something new had started slipping away. To be honest, I was becoming antsy. I was very busy and there was plenty on my plate, but nothing energized me with faith-filled excitement.

I approached the leadership team at our Monday meeting with the idea of me leaving to start another church. I explained how we could transition to another pastor more qualified to manage the next phase of New Life's growth. The leadership team unanimously opposed the idea. They did not think it was the right time or the right way to go.

I felt trapped. I had built a team on the premise that we would listen to each other and seek to navigate through major decisions together. My pioneering and entrepreneurial wiring was being overloaded by pastoral and administrative duties that seemed to weigh me down more every day. My heart sank as I tried to envision myself pastoring in that setting for another three years.

Feeling discouraged, I was listening to a tape (there once was a device called a cassette tape) by leadership guru John Maxwell. He told a short story that provided a breakthrough and spoke to me. A couple on vacation got lost in the hills of Arkansas. They happened to drive through a small town in the middle of nowhere, which consisted of a couple of houses and one small mom-and-pop store. The only person visible in the town was an old man with a long white beard smoking a pipe while he rocked back and forth on his battered rocking chair. The couple rolled down their window and asked, "Excuse us, sir. Is there anything special that this town is known for?"

The old man thought for a moment, took his pipe out of his mouth, and with a gravelly voice and country accent said, "All I know is that from this here town you can go anywhere in the world."

I don't even remember the point Maxwell was making with this story, but I do remember how this story spoke to me. It clicked inside of me that from "this here place," New Life Chicago, I could go anywhere in the world. I realized that the only thing that was limiting me was the box in which I had placed myself and the church. I didn't need to leave or move on. I simply needed to focus my energy on what I was good at where I was. From "this here town" and "this here church," we could do anything God called us to do anywhere in the world. It wasn't the church's issue; it was my issue.

> **MY PIONEERING** and entrepreneurial spirit was being overloaded by duties that seemed to weigh me down more every day.

I was most in my element when starting new ventures, casting vision, mobilizing the troops, training the team, and calling people to make decisions. I had to learn the difference between what God had called me to do and what I needed to release others to do. I needed to come to grips with the boundaries and clarity of my call.

Elijah was drained in part because he had failed to raise a team, he had taken on too much responsibility and he had not delegated. He had a solo, maverick, one-man-against-the-world syndrome. God had indeed called him to lead a spiritual counter resistance. He had chosen him to stand firm in the face of political, religious, and military opposition. But He had not chosen him to do it alone. God did not expect Elijah to take everything on himself.

Many visionary leaders are good at defining what they want to accomplish but are very poor at seeing the limits of their gifting and the boundaries of their call. They are often strong at inspiring others but weak at delegating responsibility and building a team. I have discovered that those leaders who seem to accomplish more and survive the longest are those who have developed clarity about their call and the role they play. They embrace the reality that they are not super beings and that they have limited abilities. They understand that to increase impact they must release responsibility.

Nick and Lisette have an incredible testimony. They met before either one were followers of Jesus. Lisette was a practicing Muslim and Nick was a cocky young drug dealer. They fell in love and began a stormy relationship. Lisette's parents both had a dramatic conversion and began sharing their faith with the young couple. Within a few months both Nick and Lisette had bowed their knee to the lordship of Jesus. From the beginning they developed a heart for young married couples. As they mentored couples and invested in their passion they found themselves a decade later heading up a growing marriage ministry. They asked to sit down with my wife and me.

They could not understand how they were working in the area of ministry they had a passion for but were frustrated and restless. They felt stuck. As we talked it became clear that they had a passion for married couples but they did not enjoy the administrative work involved in organizing a larger ministry. They thrived in crisis marriage intervention and short-term counseling. The mixture of passion for healthy marriages, discernment, and sensitivity to the Holy Spirit made them great at crisis intervention. When it came to organizing and managing leaders and events, though, they were drained. They felt strongly that God had called them and gifted them to work with couples but they had failed to define the boundaries of their call. They were in the right area of ministry but their focus and responsibilities were too broad.

Now Nick and Lisette have narrowed their focus to marriage crisis intervention. They meet with couples regularly and fully enjoy their clearer emphasis. Instead of being drained they have found a new energy in their call. Nick recently told me that when he and Lisette sit down with a couple that has lost hope, he feels faith and hope for them.

Not all of these hindrances to delegating and releasing will apply to every person, but you may have been able to relate to a few. I know that whatever your calling is at this juncture of your life, you are not called to do it alone. There are aspects that you will have to face by yourself and decisions that you cannot delegate, but a sustainable call always involves releasing what others can do better.

THE TRAP OF SELF-RELIANCE

Recovering clarity about our call requires understanding what we are called to do and not called to do. But it also involves understanding how we are to fulfill our call. The image of a self-reliant, independent maverick who can pull himself up by his own bootstraps is applauded in our culture. From God's perspective, however, it is the weak and the broken who have learned to rely on God who are the real heroes. Self-reliance is a subtle cancer of the soul that slowly replaces our dependence on God with our dependence on our own ability and resources. Unlike other temptations, the more experience we gain and the more successful we become, the greater becomes the lethal pull of self-reliance.

A prophet by the name of Hanani was called to challenge King Asa's self-reliance and halfhearted commitment to God. Hanani said to the king, "The eyes of the Lord move to and fro throughout the earth that He may strongly support those whose heart is completely His" (2 Chronicles 16:9 NASB).

Two things strike me about this verse. The first is the image of God systematically scouring the earth to find this rare treasure. Have you ever seen a person who has just lost a contact lens? They stop everything to search for that nearly invisible plastic disc. Their eyes move back and forth searching the floor for the elusive little lens. Now picture the all-powerful eyes of God moving back and forth as He scans the spiritual geography of earth—scanning continents, countries, provinces, cities, communities, neighborhoods, streets, and homes—until His eyes suddenly stop. A heart that is completely His is difficult to find. I picture the heavenly beings holding their breath in anticipation, and then whispering among themselves in quiet excitement, "He has found one!"

The second thing that gets my attention is what God does once He identifies this rare finding. He "strongly supports" the person whose heart is completely His (NASB). Once God finds a person whose heart is completely yielded to Him, He enjoys pouring His power into that person and demonstrating His power through that person.

But a "heart fully devoted" is not just about commitment. It's about God-reliance instead of self-reliance. King Asa, early in his life, relied on and sought after God with a sincere heart. But over the years he began to replace his dependence on God with confidence in his own experience. Years earlier when he faced a challenging military situation he went immediately to God for help and direction (2 Chronicles 14:9–13). As the years went by, Asa changed. He was more seasoned now, a veteran of political strategy and military tactics. He had built alliances and brokered difficult situations many times before. He was more sophisticated, more experienced, more developed in his leadership abilities. We would have voted him into office more quickly at this stage of his life, yet he had lost something vital. His innocent, childlike reliance upon God was gone.

King Asa's story has one of the saddest endings in all of Scripture. God allowed him to suffer military defeat and physical illness in an effort to win his heart back. Toward the end of his life, Asa's heart had become so calloused that even in his illness he did not seek God. Asa ended up stuck in his cave and never managed to find his way out. This man started with a great calling, extraordinary gifts, and leadership ability but he died just a shadow of the man he had once been. He spent his final days consulting doctors and experimenting with treatments but ignored the very God that had raised him up and had the power to heal him.

I have seen many young entrepreneurs, artists, leaders, and businesspeople derailed by the "Asa Syndrome." My own heart has pulled in that direction many times. Like a car that needs a wheel alignment, I have had to come to God, turning my back on the proud self-confidence that urges me to move forward in my own understanding and strength. How refreshing it is to open our spiritual eyes to the discovery that we can do nothing on our own of any real spiritual value. Understanding what we need to release to others and release to God are of vital importance. Clarifying our call not only involves understanding what God has called us to but what we are called to let Him handle. How liberating to transition from the hollow arrogance of self-reliance to the strength of God-dependence.

If you don't lead a ministry or a business or a nonprofit organization, you may think this principle doesn't apply to you. How can you delegate responsibility if you aren't in a position of leadership? Releasing areas that God never called you to manage applies to everyone on a personal level. Many people try to control situations and even other people they have no control over. Maybe you are stressed and anxious because you have been trying to control a grown son who is making bad choices. Maybe you are trying to change a spouse by leaving books you think they should be reading on their side of the bed—with specific pages marked and sentences highlighted. Maybe you are worried about decisions your boss is making, decisions you have no say in. Worry and anxiety are sure signs you are holding on to things God never called you to manage.

We are reminded in Philippians 4:6–7 that anxiety is not an option for a believer. "Do not be anxious about anything," Paul commands, "but in every situation, by prayer and petition, with thanksgiving, present your requests to God. And the peace of God, which transcends all understanding, will guard your hearts and your minds in Christ Jesus." Go ahead—confess to the areas in your life and work that God has not called you to carry and let them go. Letting go doesn't mean you don't care anymore. It simply means you care enough to let God handle what you cannot. A new season of life awaits you, if you are ready to embrace the future God has for you.

CHAPTER 10

TAKE THE FIRST STEP

The Mexican policeman in dark sunglasses leaned in closer to my car window. He rested his hand on his revolver, and asked a question that shocked me. I did a double take and asked somewhat confused, "Excuse me, what did you just say?"

I was speaking at a conference in San Diego, and I asked some friends to come along to enjoy the Southern California weather for a weekend. After the conference my friend John had an idea. He and his wife had never crossed the border into Mexico and were excited to take advantage of the opportunity. We decided to cross the border for the afternoon and have lunch at a seafood place near Tijuana.

We went to the nearest car rental office to lease a car for the day. The attendant advised me to be careful crossing the border. "Once you cross the border it's a different world," he warned. He related how just the week before a couple had rented a vehicle to do the same thing we were doing. The local police in Tijuana stopped them and ordered them out of the car. The police entered their car and proceeded to drive off, leaving the couple stranded on the side of the road. We thanked the attendant and promised to be careful. Six of us drove in the minivan across the border with no incident. We enjoyed an authentic meal at a quaint Mexican restaurant near the ocean. We finished our meal, strolled around the town, and enjoyed a relaxing afternoon. When it was time to head back, I drove the van back toward the border crossing.

We were in a lively conversation, laughing and joking, when one of the passengers said, "Hey, there's a policeman following you."

I laughed and said, "Yeah, right." I adjusted my mirror and saw a Mexican motorcycle policeman following closely behind me. I put my turn signal on and casually switched lanes. The policeman followed right behind me. Then, to the dismay of everyone in our van, he starting flashing his lights and motioning us to pull over. I reluctantly pulled to the side of the road. The officer dismounted his motorcycle and approached the driver's side window. He wore a helmet and dark sunglasses, and a revolver hung from a holster on his hip.

He looked first at me and then glanced at the other passengers in the vehicle before he ordered me to pull into the side street ahead. As I pulled onto the side road my passengers warned me to be careful and to be ready to take off if necessary. The officer asked for my documentation matter-of-factly. He said he was going to have to take me down to the police station to pay a fine, because I had been speeding a few miles down the road. I expressed my surprise that he couldn't simply write me a ticket. He shook his head ominously. He continued to ask questions and stall for time, as if he were waiting for me to offer him a bribe. When I told him I was a pastor in Chicago, he paused and looked at me seriously. Then he said something that caught me totally off guard.

This Mexican policeman in dark sunglasses leaned in closer to my window, rested his hand on his revolver, and asked me somberly, "What does Romans 13 say?"

I did a double take. I wasn't sure I had heard him correctly. "Excuse me, sir, what did you just say?"

"What does Romans 13 say?" he repeated.

Two thoughts immediately raced through my mind. First was, *What in the world* does *Romans 13 say? Second was, If I don't pass this Bible quiz I may end up in a Mexican prison.* I fumbled for words, stalling for time to remember Romans 13. "Well," I said, "Romans 12 tells us not to be conformed to this world."

He looked at me and it was obvious he was not impressed.

Then I remembered the general gist of Romans 13. I blurted out, "Romans 13 says to submit to the governing authorities since they are servants of God." He immediately took off his sunglasses and shook my hand. For the rest of our conversation, he referred to me as "pastor." He told me to watch the way I drive and be careful in this town. As he walked back to his motorcycle, I sat stunned. He rode his motorcycle up beside my car and said, "Pastor, tell your congregation in Chicago to pray for the police department in Tijuana. We really need it." Then he rode off.

I buckled my seat belt, looked in the rearview mirror, and carefully pulled away. It dawned on me that I had crossed the border into a different country and culture, but God was not limited by human borders. He had given me the tools to move to the next territory without going to jail. What are the chances that a guy from Chicago would speak Spanish and know what Romans 13 says?

Some of you reading these pages are standing at the edge of your cave and contemplating your first step across the border. I want to remind you that God has already gone before you. Stepping out of the cave may stretch your faith, but God is already preparing a way.

The first step out never comes without challenges. Crossing borders, stepping into new seasons, walking through open doors will always stretch our faith and challenge our comfort. The moment you step out of the cave into a new environment the adventure begins.

THE CHAIN REACTION

When God calls Elijah out of his cave in 1 Kings 19:15, He says to him, "Go back the way you came." He tells Elijah He has prepared colleagues, a confidant, and a community for the prophet. Verse 19 records Elijah's response: "So Elijah went from there."

It's a small phrase but it carries tremendous implications. This marks the point of action. The powerful encounter with the wind, earthquake, and fire plus the profound whisper of God was all leading up to this moment. Not only did Elijah have to choose to leave the cave behind, but he also had to choose to leave the cave in the right direction. Elijah had only been physically stuck in a cave for a short time, but he had been traveling down a spiritually and emotionally destructive road for almost a month and a half. Behind this first step are weeks of wrestling with God, himself, and his call. His first step unleashed a chain reaction that affected Elijah body, soul, and spirit.

Stepping out of your personal cave always involves a bold step that begins with a simple choice. The chain reaction that led us into the cave has to be reversed on our way out. Elijah was dragged into the cave when fear gripped his soul, pulled his body down to exhaustion, and dragged his spirit to spiritual backsliding.

In June 1981, sixteen mountain climbers who were roped together for safety fell more than 2,000 feet down an Oregon mountain slope called Cooper Spur. Five of the climbers were killed and four more were severely injured as they attempted to climb an 11,000-foot mountain. One of the surviving climbers said that someone in the team fell first and dragged the rest of the climbers down with them. The ropes that tied them together were meant to serve as a safeguard, but instead they became their downfall.

In a similar way, our personal being is tied together in three parts: spirit, soul, and body. In his first letter to the believers in Thessalonica, Paul says, "May your whole spirit, soul and body be kept blameless at the coming of our Lord Jesus Christ" (1 Thessalonians 5:23). These three are deeply connected to one another. Each one of these parts of our person can hold the others up but can also pull the others down. Like the young woman who spiraled down emotionally over the breakup of a boyfriend. Her frail emotional state began to affect her body so much that she became very ill. Her desperate emotions dragged down her body and ended up pulling her spiritual life right down with them. She began to feel like God was far off and distant and her spiritual life plummeted as well. In retrospect, her downward spiral started with her soul that dragged her body down and ended up pulling her spirit down as well. In a short amount of time this vibrant young woman was in a dark pit of despondency, overwhelmed physically, emotionally, and spiritually. Like the Oregon mountain climbers, every part of her being came crashing down.

Some people have been crippled so long that it has warped their whole person. The gospel of Luke introduces us to a woman who was stuck for eighteen long years. For almost two decades she was bent over with severe curvature of her spine so crippling that her daily activities were a constant challenge. No doubt eating, drinking, and even walking were extremely difficult. Constant pain was her everyday companion. Children pointed at her and asked out loud, "Mom, what's wrong with that lady?" Her relationships, her finances, her health, her identity, her spiritual state were all deeply affected by her condition.

Dr. Ralph F. Wilson says this disease is probably what physicians today would call Marie-Strümpell Disease, a fusion of the spinal bones. Sufferers often find "that the pain is relieved somewhat when they lean forward. So they often go through the day leaning slightly forward, and gradually their spine begins to fuse. The more they lean in order to relieve the pain, the greater the angle, until a patient might be bent almost double,"[1] as is the lady in this account. This disease is a chronic and progressive form of arthritis distinguished by inflammation and stiffness and in some patients even ossification of joints especially in the lower spine.

While her medical issue was undeniably physical, the root of her problem was spiritual. She had a spiritual problem that affected her soul and her body as well. Luke, the author of this gospel and the book of Acts, was also a doctor. And he uses interesting words to diagnose her condition. He doesn't use the word that would mean "illness, disease, or injury." Instead he uses the phrase "crippled by a spirit."

Scripture says, "When Jesus saw her, he called her forward" (Luke 13:12). Her journey to freedom hinged on her willingness to take the difficult step of responding to the promptings of Jesus. This is one of the most important details in this moving passage. And if you read it quickly you can miss it altogether. *Jesus called her forward.* No one with a deformity of any kind wants to step up to the public platform. Jesus is calling a deformed woman out of shadows of her own personal cave into the spotlight. This is a difficult moment, but she responds and takes the first painful step forward. She has to leave the comfort of her cave and take the risk of stepping into an uncertain future.

"Woman, you are set free from your infirmity," Jesus clearly says. "Then he put his hands on her, and immediately she straightened up and praised God" (Luke 13:12–13).

This woman's journey to wholeness of body, soul, and spirit began with one bold step forward. Her first step took her out of the shadows and into the vulnerability of her greatest insecurities.

So many of us stop at the entrance of the cave. We remain in the coolness of the cave putting off our first bold step. We are so close but yet remain so far until we take the step. Elijah stood at the entrance of his cave feeling the same way. He knew that one step out of the cave meant he would have to obey the directives of God and go back the way he came. He would be forced to face his greatest fears and deepest insecurities. All of us who are stuck have to wrestle with that first important step.

ONCE YOU ARE STRETCHED, YOU CAN'T GO BACK

In 1995, New Life had reached a crossroads in our journey as a congregation. Outwardly things seemed good. We had outgrown several buildings. We were attracting people from many parts of the city of Chicago. We were expanding, reaching people for God, and starting new ministries. But I had a growing sense that we were not quite on course, that we were spiritually plateaued. One day, one of our pastors handed me a book called *This Coming Revival* by Campus Crusade leader Bill Bright. Bright was looking for two million believers to fast and pray forty days for spiritual awakening in America. I presented the challenge to our pastoral team and we all decided to fast together. Many people from the congregation joined in some form of fasting during that time and all together about twenty-five of us committed to the entire forty days. We followed Bright's fasting prescription, which allowed for water and fruit juices but no food.

The first week of a fast is the hardest, and this one was no exception. But we were motivated to seek God and press through for a spiritual breakthrough. Toward the end, my energy was low. I lost forty pounds. My wife bemoaned that several of us looked like concentration-camp survivors. But we were having a powerful season of private and corporate prayer.

As the final day of the fast approached, I decided that I would spend the last twenty-four hours at a local hotel with my Bible, seeking God in solitude. After thirty-nine days of concentrated prayer, repentance, and seeking God, praise seemed to come easily and prayer flowed unhindered. My spirit felt unusually sensitive and the Scripture seemed to explode with meaning and insight.

Soon I found myself interceding for the people of Chicago. I cried out for the city and the millions of people who desperately needed to know the love of Christ. I pictured the city from a satellite view and pleaded for the different communities of this metropolis. My cries gave way to a somber silence as I lay facedown on my hotel bed. I lay there quietly for several moments. "Give me one percent of Chicago," I heard myself pray out loud. The moment I prayed this prayer I knew something unusual had happened. I slowly prayed it again. The heavy burden I had felt for the city suddenly lifted. I sensed somehow that the entire fast had been leading up to that point. Immediately I had the courage and faith to pray that little prayer with greater boldness. I walked out of that hotel entrance pregnant with a vision.

At home I found a calculator and did the math. One percent of a population of three million is 30,000 people. I almost fell off my chair when I wrote 30,000 on a piece of paper. I scheduled a meeting with our leadership team. I wrote this question on the board: "What would a church of 30,000 people look like in Chicago?" We wrote several observations that in time would almost seem prophetic. They are summarized in this vision statement:

> God has called us to nurture and build a church that models community, spearheads prayer, leads the way in multi-racial and cross-cultural ministry, is energetic and intentional about making disciples, is a Kingdom bridge-builder, trains and mobilizes people into ministry, has a heart for the poor and needy, and spreads throughout Chicagoland by planting life-giving communities of faith and spiritually vibrant small groups.

When I was a kid we played a game to see who could blow the biggest balloon. The goal was to blow up the largest balloon without it popping. I noticed that once my balloon had been inflated to capacity it would never go back to its original size. Even when all the air is let out of the balloon it is not the same, because it has been stretched beyond repair. A God-sized vision has the same effect on a church and people. After that season of fasting and prayer ended, I could not go back to normal. I had been stretched by a vision and something had changed. Once God had stretched us with a vision of reaching

30,000 people that could potentially transform the spiritual landscape of Chicago, we could no longer be the church we had been. Once your soul has been stretched by a God-given vision, it can never return to its original size.

Many people have visions and dreams and live at the edge of their cave. But the hard steps are where we all get stuck. As a church we had to take the hard step of releasing leaders, groups of people, and resources to start new campuses around the city. The first time we launched a group of people to another community, I had to force myself to celebrate on the outside, but I mourned on the inside. I knew it was the right step but it was difficult to release close friends. We struggled with feeling like we did not have enough leaders, sufficient finances, or enough expertise to move forward. I have never known a person or organization moving out of a cave that doesn't feel nervous or uncertain about the future.

"GIVE ME ONE percent of Chicago," I heard myself pray out loud.

As I write these words we are planning the launch of our twentieth church campus in Chicago. Because we took that first step we now have congregations in nineteen different communities with thirty-five worship services that minister to thousands of people each week. In the last three years we have baptized over a thousand people who found new life in God all over the city of Chicago. The season of being stuck led to a season of fasting and prayer that led to fresh vision that led to taking action steps that has led to thousands of people being impacted.

It always starts with a first bold step.

TIME FOR A BOLD STEP

Over the past decade I have helped lead encounter retreats for both men and women. Hundreds of people attended these weekend retreats each year that focus on walking in freedom. Each year we end the retreat by asking those attending to write down the bold steps they will take once they leave the retreat. Many of them publicly announce their bold step before walking through "victors lane" where supporters high-five them and shout words of encouragement. The best bold steps have several things in common.

- ▶ They are always difficult to take and usually involve facing a major fear. Let's be honest. If it were easy you would have taken this step a long time ago.
- ▶ They are written down and shared with others. Accountability assures that we will follow through.
- ▶ They are concrete. The best bold steps are the ones you know you have taken or have not taken. There is no ambiguity.
- ▶ They have an expiration date. If our steps have no deadlines, we will be tempted to procrastinate. We can deceive ourselves into thinking we will eventually follow through while we put things off indefinitely. Remember, delayed obedience is ultimately disobedience.
- ▶ They are the first step in a longer journey.

The journey out of the cave is different for everyone but here are some of the steps that I have heard:

I am going to gather my three children and apologize for not being the father God has called me to be.

I am going to propose to the woman I should have married several years ago.

I am going to call my father and release him from the bitterness I have held against him for fifteen years.

I am going to join a twelve-step group and finally deal with my addiction.

I'm going to break up with my boyfriend who is not a believer and is not God's best for my life.

I am going home to wash my wife's feet and ask her to forgive me for not being a servant leader.

I am cutting up my credit cards and declaring a war on debt.

I am taking the step of baptism and boldly stepping into my new life in Christ.

Our challenge is not simply to emerge from the cave, but to step out of the cave a changed person. Every new season requires a fresh sense of power and spiritual influence to succeed in. Elijah stepped boldly out of the cave toward the dreaded desert but with a new expectation. He had been changed by the cave. What bold step do you need to take?

CHAPTER 11

AVOID A RELAPSE

Jimmy was struggling. He had battled a severe heroin addiction for many years. He started attending New Life and expressed a sincere desire to follow God and turn his life around. After a meeting I asked Jimmy how he was doing. He lowered his head and said, "It has been hard. I want to change, but I have lived this way for so many years."

I asked him, "Are you ready to do whatever it takes to change?"

He looked up at me and said, "I am willing to do anything—whatever it takes this time."

I surprised myself when I said, "Pack your bags and move into my house until you get on your feet."

He looked at me in disbelief and said, "I'm not sure I can do that."

I double-checked with my wife, and Jimmy reluctantly moved in the next day. He was a few years older than I, but he had aged prematurely because of his long years of addiction. In spite of his age he soon felt like an older son to Dee and me. We lived in a building with three apartments, and each of the three couples living in the building had made a commitment to try to live out our Christianity on our block. We had decided to open our home to people who were hurting and in need until they could manage on their own. Jimmy moved into our spare bedroom and slowly started to get used to living in his new setting. He had a likeable personality and a sincere desire to move beyond his rocky history. Each morning we made sure Jimmy joined us in a time of prayer and reading Scripture.

For the first couple of weeks he wrestled with withdrawal and the struggle of living drug free, but soon he was feeling healthy in his newfound sobriety. I asked him to start filling out job applications so that he would not have so much time on his hands. Jimmy was making progress in his walk with God and in his responsibilities as a man. We helped him study for a test to work for the City of Chicago, and to our amazement he passed with an excellent grade. Soon Jimmy had a steady job and a decent paycheck. He had some dental work done to repair the damage to his teeth from years of drug abuse, so even his contagious smile was back. He began to look healthier, gained some needed weight, and put on a uniform to go to his job each day. His extended family was ecstatic that finally, after years of struggling, Jimmy was getting back on his feet.

After about six months he felt it was time to live on his own, so we helped him move to his new place and prayed over him when he left. It seemed like Jimmy had graduated to a new season of independent living. He did well for a season, but gradually we began seeing him less and less. Slowly he started to lose that humble, cautious attitude and dependence on God that had helped him move forward at first. Jimmy started to slack off in the disciplines that had helped him get out of his cave when he felt so desperate. He began skipping his recovery meetings and not making it to his Bible study group. He excused his absence by saying he was working a lot of hours, but assured us that he was still doing well.

Time passed. Jimmy moved and did not leave a forwarding address. I heard that he had moved in with a girlfriend but did not know much more. It was a couple of years before I received any news about Jimmy. A mutual friend called to inform me that Jimmy had started to frequent some of the old hangouts again. He had gotten sucked into his old lifestyle and lost his job. He had quickly slipped back into his addiction. Within a short time, he was living out on the streets again. My friend paused over the phone, "I'm sorry to tell you this, but Jimmy contracted AIDS and died last week after days in a coma." My heart sank when I heard the news. I knew what Jimmy could have been if he would have stayed unstuck. I knew this was not the end that God had purposed for Jimmy.

Not everyone's relapse is as tragic as Jimmy's, but no one can assume that their exit from the cave is permanent. Living out our call from one season to the next without getting stuck requires putting into practice what we have learned from our cave experience.

Besides the challenge of initially getting unstuck, most of us face the equally difficult challenge of how to remain unstuck. The circumstances, habits, and thinking that led us to get stuck in the first place still tug at us once we have left the cave. The single mother who has finally managed to eliminate financial debt will need to continue to guard against the habits that lead back to the hole of indebtedness. The man who has managed to lose those difficult twenty-five pounds will have to continue to exercise to stay fit. The woman who has finally been able to forgive her ex-husband will need to fight to maintain that attitude of release. That college student who has pulled out of the rut of spiritual apathy will need to fan the flame to maintain his spiritual vitality.

Elijah was never the same after his cave experience. He had encountered his own frailty and yet been exposed to the manifest presence of God. He had tasted the darkness of the cave yet had been called out by the voice of his Creator. After the cave, Elijah lived as a man who knew God at a deeper level. He seemed to walk in the knowledge of the Holy.

And he never returned to his cave again.

In fact Elijah goes on to finish his life with unmatched strength, authority, and passion. After the cave:

- ▶ He boldly raises his prophetic voice against King Ahab and brings the king to his knees in broken repentance.
- ▶ He challenges Ahaziah (Ahab's son and successor) and pronounces judgment on his entire household.
- ▶ He calls fire down from heaven on two separate occasions as he stands in defiance to the misguided king Ahaziah.
- ▶ He leads the school of the prophets with a status that is unequaled.
- ▶ He flows with such power that he rolls up his mantle and divides the waters of the Jordan.

▶ He grants his successor, Elisha, the opportunity to inherit a double portion of the Spirit.

▶ He walks with such intimate connection with God that he knows the exact time of His departure.

▶ He is taken out of this world in the most dramatic ascension recorded in Scripture.

Needless to say, Elijah finished well. The cave experience changed him and launched him into a new season of his life.

"DO YOU WANT TO GET WELL?"

I have noticed that many times when we are stuck, we sincerely desire to move on but often spend our time looking for solutions in the wrong places. We passively wait for our circumstances to change. We look to the stirring of the water when the One with power to change our destiny is walking by.

One of the most vivid images of being stuck is found in John chapter 5. We read of a pool of water called Bethesda. The sick, blind, lame, and paralyzed would camp out around this pool. In later manuscripts a commentator added that the sick believed that an angel would stir the water, and the first to enter would be healed. While others were living their lives, going to work, building houses, marrying, and having children, the Bethesda people would lie there with other stuck people, waiting and hoping for something to change.

Jesus passed by the pool and noticed a paralyzed man by the edge of the water. Someone told Jesus that this man had been in this condition for thirty-eight years. Something about this man drew the attention of Jesus. Maybe it was the fact that he had been stuck so long, or that his condition seemed so desperate, or that his desire to get unstuck was so sincere.

With compassion in His eyes and authority in His voice, Jesus asked this paralyzed man a strange question, "Do you want to get well?" (John 5:6).

This seems like a peculiar question to ask a sick person who spends his life beside a pool waiting for the water to be magically stirred. Often Jesus challenges the obvious. Some people have lived so long with an old problem that they prefer it to a new solution. This man's friends, culture, environment, and identity for thirty-eight years had been wrapped up in his paralysis. Healing would be a radical change not only to his body, but to his world.

"Do you want to get well?" is the question Jesus poses to this man stuck for over three decades.

Getting unstuck and staying unstuck has to do with making a choice. Do we really want to get unstuck? This paralyzed man did not answer the question that Jesus asked him. Instead he explains why he is still stuck. " 'Sir,' the invalid replied, 'I have no one to help me into the pool when the water is stirred. While I am trying to get in, someone else goes down ahead of me' " (v. 7). Many of us, when we are stuck, cover up or avoid dealing with our problem in various ways: denial, generalizing, minimizing, blaming, excusing, dodging, and attacking others. There comes a time when we are challenged to stop making excuses for being stuck and stop waiting around for circumstances to change and simply say "Yes" to God.

Without any further discussion Jesus said, " 'Get up! Pick

up your mat and walk.' At once the man was cured; he picked up his mat and walked" (vv. 8–9). This must have been an incredible moment. The other stuck men and women were looking at the pool of water when they should have been looking at Jesus. Their heads were turned in the wrong direction. The power to transform them was right before them but they missed it because they were waiting for chance or luck to change their life.

This man who had not walked in thirty-eight years rises to his feet, picks up his mat, and walks away from the pool of stuck living.

For years when I read this passage, it puzzled me why Jesus would command the paralytic to "pick up [his] mat." It seems out of place that at this dramatic moment Jesus would mention the mat. Who cares about an old, dirty mat when legs are about to be brought to life again? If it were me, I would want to shove the old mat in the trash and never look at it again. He had spent countless hours on that mat. That mat was his old home and it held his place next to the pool. He had literally lived on this mat by day and slept on it at night. I believe there is something symbolic in the command to pick up his mat. Implicit in the command is, "You are never coming back to this place again." He was no longer going to save his place in line for the pool or mark his territory. Picking up his mat was leaving the old completely behind.

My first winter in Chicago, I was struck by a curious neighborhood ritual. I was driving through the neighborhood after a major snowstorm and I noticed old chairs, stools, cones, plastic crates, and even an old tricycle strategically placed along the street. I discovered that after you spend thirty minutes shoveling snow in the frigid cold to clear a parking area, you want to make sure no one else takes your space. That old chair on the street tells other people, "This is my spot; don't mess with it." A young friend of mine moved a chair last winter when he could not find a parking space. When he came back, his car window had been smashed. In Chicago, you don't mess with people's parking spots. That old chair means I will return to this spot soon. Leaving that old mat beside the pool would have sent the message, "Keep my spot. I may have to return to this place again."

Like the woman who boldly declares that she is done with prescription tranquilizers but still keeps the half empty bottle in the back of the kitchen drawer. She is saying, "I hope this works, but if it doesn't, I'm saving my spot." Or the man who determines this time that an unhealthy relationship is in the past and he will never go back but still keeps his ex-girlfriend's number on speed dial in his phone. If you keep the mat beside the old pool you are giving yourself the option of returning.

When Jesus saw the man again He warned him, "See, you are well again. Stop sinning or something worse may happen to you" (v. 14). Jesus was pointing out that the behaviors that led to his condition in the first place could lead him right back there again. Relapse to the cave is all too common. The lessons we take away from our cave experience need to be ingrained in our soul to avoid a relapse.

"I'M NOT GOING TO MAKE THE SAME MISTAKE AGAIN"

All of us can be pulled back to the cave that we stepped out of. Those who resist the pull and refuse to return are those that revisit the lessons they have learned. Those who stay acutely aware of their relapse potential stop and remember. They remember how they got stuck, how they felt when they were stuck, and what they learned in the process of getting unstuck.

My younger son, Grant, has always been adventurous. By the time he was six years old he had already broken four bones and received stitches on his head. As I write he is recovering from a knee surgery due to an injury this year on the freshman high school football team. His need to push himself physically and the thrill of risk have led him to try various sports. A few years ago we were at an indoor rock-climbing wall. He had climbed all the walls indicated for his age, but he wanted more of a challenge. So he climbed numerous walls, each escalating in difficulty. Finally he reached the most difficult level. By this time, he was tired and I was ready to go home. I agreed to let him climb the final wall. With determination he looked to the top of the wall and started climbing. As he climbed I could tell this was going to be a real challenge. He slowly made his way up the wall, reaching, stretching, and finding footholds. Several times I thought he would fall, but he maintained his grip. He climbed two-thirds of the way up and then stopped moving. He was stuck. His arms were too short to reach the next ledge. There was nowhere for his feet to go in order to move higher. He tried multiple angles, but it was apparent he was at a dead end.

In one final attempt, he lunged at the next ledge. His hands slipped and he dangled in the air, saved by his harness. As I lowered him to the ground I said, "Well you gave it a good shot. Nice try." Undeterred, he insisted on attempting the climb again. This time he tried a different path. He reached the same height and was stuck again. I watched him once again cling to the rock with the tip of his fingers. His arms were shaking with exhaustion and once again he fell and dangled in his harness. "Okay, that's it," I said. "This is a tough wall. I think you need to tackle it when you are a little older."

"No, Dad!" he said. "I think I know how to reach the top this time." He looked up at the wall and said, "I know how I got stuck. I'm not going to make the same mistake again." He pointed to a new ledge and said, "I can make it that way." With determination in his eyes and armed with a new plan birthed from the failure of his two previous attempts, he started climbing. When he finally made it to the top, he looked down with a big smile and gave me a thumbs-up.

Today, pause and remember what led you to get stuck in the first place. Like Grant, if you climb that same route you will end up in the same place. Remember the route, remember the pain, and remember what you learned.

CHAPTER 12

BREATHE THE AIR OF A NEW SEASON

The pilot cleared his voice and announced over the intercom that there were problems with landing. "I have good news and bad news," he said.

You don't want to hear the pilot of a 747 say in midair that he has bad news.

"The bad news is that we cannot land in Barajas Airport in Madrid," he said. "The good news is that Charles de Gaulle airport in Paris has opened a runway, so we can land in Paris." Passengers throughout the airplane groaned in disappointment. Under other circumstances I might have enjoyed being rerouted to Paris. But my wife was not with me and I was scheduled to speak at a conference the next day. I was about to be stuck in France when I was supposed to be speaking in Spain.

All the air traffic controllers in Spain went on strike the day we were scheduled to fly into Madrid. According to *The New*

TODAY, PAUSE and remember what led you to get stuck in the first place.

York Times, in that forty-eight-hour period, 4,300 flights were canceled, affecting approximately 600,000 passengers. The Spanish government declared a state of emergency and authorized the military to take over traffic control operations.[1]

Of course, we didn't know any of that at the time. I was traveling on a tight schedule with two young leaders from Chicago to speak at a conference in Madrid, and now we were going to be stuck "indefinitely" in France. I was sure we would never make it in time.

I called and apologetically informed the conference organizer that I was stuck and he better have a backup plan. After checking in to the hotel, my traveling team convinced me to take a taxi to downtown Paris to see some sights. One of the other passengers we met, an architect from New York, heard us talking and asked if he could join us. During the taxi ride downtown we were bemoaning the fact that we were all missing important appointments. The architect was supposed to attend a wedding that he now would most likely miss. We were stuck hundreds of miles away from where we were supposed to be with no idea when we would be able to resume our journey. But as we walked around downtown Paris it dawned on me that God may have a purpose in our being stuck.

After a quick visit to the top of the Eiffel Tower, we ended up at a corner café in a quaint Parisian neighborhood with our new friend. After placing our order the architect asked, "So what do you do for a living?" I told him I was a pastor in Chicago. He looked at me somewhat startled. By now I am used to this reaction. Like many people, I just assumed he started rewinding our conversation to remember how much colorful language and how many expletives he had used before he knew I was a pastor.

Instead he looked at me and said, "You are not going to believe this, but I just said to the Man Upstairs that I needed a sign on this trip so I would know He was still there. I am not much of a praying man," he confessed, "but lately I have been going through a crisis and looking to the heavens for answers." He explained, "My son is like you guys. In fact he is a youth minister." He confided, "My son just told me that he and his wife were skipping meals for a few days to pray for me." As we talked I discovered to my surprise that I had recently met his son. What are the chances? He was from New Jersey and I was from Chicago, and we had met in Dallas at a small gathering of people in ministry.

The fact that he was stranded in Paris with a pastor who knew his son who was currently praying for him got my new friend's attention. We ended up talking at length with this New York architect about God, the gospel, and destiny. When we returned to the hotel I asked if we could pray for him. So there we were in a hotel lobby in Paris praying over an architect from New York. When we finished praying he had tears in his eyes. I told him, "God must really love you to reroute hundreds of passengers and get us all stuck in the same hotel so your prayer for a sign could be answered."

The next morning we learned that the strike had been canceled and that we would be flying out to Spain immediately.

We made it to our conference on time. More important, I was reminded that even when I am stuck, God is always doing something behind the scenes. I just need to open my eyes and look.

TOOLS FOR THE NEXT SEASON

All of us are being equipped in the present for the calling and the challenges we will face in the future. God is systematically adding the tools in your tool belt that you will need, even before you know you need them. When I review my story I am amazed at how God seems to have handcrafted certain experiences to uniquely prepare me for the setting in which I now find myself. Of course, in the moment I always wondered why I am going through the challenge or personal headache, only to discover later that a slot in my tool belt has been filled through that difficult experience.

Elijah's cave experience was the crisis that prepared him for the next season of his life and ministry. He left the cave with a fresh vision, a new strategy, and the name of his successor. The journey to the cave was the most painful and the darkest season of Elijah's life. But he exited that cave with clear directives from God. His apprentice and successor, Elisha, would be the direct beneficiary of the lessons Elijah learned in that cave. Elijah's cave experience ensured a legacy that outlasted his own life and continued through his successors.

Every person who is currently stuck in a cave is being called out by the voice of God. God wants to place on your tool belt the tools you need for the next season of your life. He is the great redeemer of our cave experiences. Every cave experience you have can be recaptured for a purpose. Be prepared to discover a divine purpose every time you allow yourself to get stuck.

In his book *The Advantage,* business consultant Patrick Lencioni tells a story that illustrates this point from an episode of *I Love Lucy*:

> Ricky, Lucy's husband, comes home from work one day to find his wife crawling around the living room on her hands and knees. He asks her what she's doing. "I'm looking for my earrings," Lucy responds. Ricky asks her, "You lost your earrings in the living room?" She shakes her head. "No, I lost them in the bedroom. But the light out here is much better."[2]

Like Lucy, Lencioni says, many people look for answers where the light is better and where they are most comfortable. But that's not where we find what we need. It is in the darkness of the cave, as we search our soul and ask the hard questions, that we come away with answers for our next season.

I don't know what your cave looks like or how long you have been there, but I do know that it doesn't have to be your final destination. In fact some of us will look back and eventually thank God for the gift of the cave. The cave can become a major turning point in our lives. Here are two stories that will help you see caves as an unexpected gift. I hope they will inspire you to believe God for your new season beyond the cave.

THE GIFT OF THE CAVE

Bill was on the fast track to success. From a young boy he had a desire to win and a drive to succeed. During college he had the natural ability but lacked the discipline to work hard and pursue his dreams. Four years in the army taught him the power of sheer discipline and determination. Within a few years back in the workplace, Bill was quickly climbing the business ladder. Not afraid to risk and hungry to succeed, he threw himself into becoming a millionaire. For a season it seemed like everything Bill touched turned to gold. He built up a profitable employment business that was doing well and growing. A new partner assured Bill that this was the time to expand aggressively. Armed with a new sense of confidence and the expertise of his new partner he launched seventy new branches of his company.

The dream seemed to be coming together before his very eyes. He felt unstoppable. The economic optimism of the 1990s was in full swing and Bill was riding the wave. From 1997 to 2000 the Internet bubble was swelling exponentially and companies were turning a rapid profit and Bill was right in the middle of it. Then the unexpected happened. The dot-com bubble burst, sending waves of panic and a dramatic downturn in the economy. Some companies came crashing down quickly. Others suffered major loss as their stock plummeted. Practically every portion of the economy was stunned. At the end of the year 2000 *The New York Times* reported, "What a difference a year makes. The Nasdaq sank. Stock tips have been replaced with talk of recession. Many pioneering dot-coms are out of business or barely surviving. The Dow Jones Internet Index, made up of dot-com blue chips, is down more than 72 percent since March."[3]

Bill had expanded aggressively right before the bubble burst. Over the twelve months his company went from employing four hundred fifty people down to a hundred. For months Bill struggled on the verge of bankruptcy. His world had come crashing down and he had nowhere else to turn. Bill had a faith background but was nominal at best. In the midst of his crisis, in desperation, he visited a Christian church. He found solace in the praise songs he heard and felt strangely comforted sitting in the back pew of the church. Bill had been stuck for years in a cycle of materialism where his god had become work and success. People around him applauded him for his apparent golden touch but deep within Bill knew something was missing.

Bill's first step out of the cave was in the midst of a two-year financial crisis where his economic survival was uncertain. Bill set a meeting with the pastor to explain his story and get some counsel. Bill recently told me, "The phrase that got my attention in my darkest period was, 'Jesus must really love you to put you through this.' It made me realize that Jesus had a purpose for my life, and He wanted my attention." It was in the midst of crisis that Bill surrendered his life to God and understood the gospel of Jesus Christ clearly for the first time. He stepped out of his spiritual cave but his circumstances were as bad, or worse, than they had been. Even after his decision to surrender to God, every week seemed to bring a near economic collapse. Each day continued to be a struggle to survive but Bill found an unusual peace that amazed him and the people around him.

Stepping out of our cave does not mean that the clouds part and the glory of God shines through opening every door and dissolving every problem. Sometimes we step out of the cave into the most trying time of our life. A change of season does not necessarily mean a change of circumstances. It *does* mean an internal change that allows us to live in line with our call in the midst of our personal storm. Nelson Mandela, after twenty-seven years of imprisonment, said when he was released, "There is nothing like returning to a place that remains unchanged to find the ways in which you yourself have altered."

Miraculously, after a two-year period Bill finally turned a corner in his business. His priorities and life had taken a dramatic turn a year and a half earlier. Bill recently confided that he is now ten times more successful financially than he was before he entered his life-changing crisis, but that is little compared to the new season of purpose and peace with God he is now living. He has found his new mission as he continues in business but looks for opportunities to speak into the lives of other businesspeople still trying to find their identity in success and achievement. Bill is a businessman who has found his call. Bill discovered in the crisis of his cave a great gift from God.

BULLETS AND TATTOOS

Vince was from the other side of the tracks but needed to break out of his cave just as much as Bill did. On April 3 at 2:00

a.m., Vince was on the corner of 51st and Wood on Chicago's Southwest side. He was hanging out in opposing gang territory partying with some friends. A Chevy pulled off the main street. Its lights were off, the telltale sign of a drive-by.

Vince heard tires screech to a stop and saw the blur of a backseat passenger lean out the window at point-blank range. He was instantly on edge with nowhere to hide.

"The first shot was shocking, the blast was loud, and close. It happened so fast," Vince says, "then everything switched to slow motion." Then another shot only a few feet away made him jump. "My right hand flew up into the air from the impact; my left hand instinctively threw a gang sign. Then my right arm fell back down to my side and wouldn't move," Vince said. He swore as he glared to the sky and screamed toward heaven, "You just won't quit, God, will You!"

The tattooed cross on his forearm was shredded to pieces by the bullet's impact. The slug tore through the center of his forearm, split into eight pieces and exited the other side. Vince felt searing pain and he began to bleed profusely.

At the emergency room the doctor had a devastating prognosis for Vince: amputation. "I felt as if God was going to take my right arm to get back at me, to humiliate me. It was worse than death in my mind," Vince says. This would be the ultimate retaliation from God. Weakness for everyone to see, and he would have to live with it for the rest of his life.

Right-handed and only sixteen years old. *What will I do with my life?* Vince thought. He had nowhere to turn, and no one to turn to. "I was cornered, and desperate. I knew I had no options," Vince says. "There was only one who had the power

WHEN VINCE got shot he screamed toward heaven, "You just won't quit, God, will You!"

to help me now, but why would He?"

Vince whispered a desperate prayer. "God, if You exist, and if You care, help me believe by saving my arm!" Minutes later, the amputation was canceled. The doctors had changed their minds. They put a cast on Vince's arm, but his prayer was quickly forgotten. Soon Vince was back on the streets and now his focus was revenge.

"When they shoot you in the arm, you shoot them in the head—that's the gang mindset," Vince says. "But I couldn't shoot. My arm was all but dead." No feeling, no movement. And no hope of recovery. Any time he looked at his right arm, he recoiled in anger—anger he couldn't follow through on.

A year passed. As Vince struggled to make sense of his injury, gang life quickly sucked him back in. Still violent, still angry, still empty. Nothing had really changed in his world except now he was crippled. He was still in the gang, still enraged, still confused. He was still stuck in his dark cave. He still hated God. Yes, everything seemed the same. Until one day.

Vince's finger twitched.

The movement was very small. More like a little jerk. Vince was shocked when it happened. Against all odds, his hand had moved. He rushed to the doctor. Again, a slight move, but in front of the doctor who realized he had witnessed the impossible.

"Here was a trained medical professional, a doctor, and he started crying," Vince says. "He told me, 'I'm not a religious man, but if I were you, I would start going to church and thanking the Man Upstairs.' "

This was the moment. After a lifetime of pain and horror, where God had a ringside seat, Vince suddenly saw God in a way he hadn't seen Him before. Vince suddenly realized that God had done more than simply answer his prayer to prevent the amputation. Instead, God had done what no doctor could do. God had worked a miracle.

In the months that followed, Vince began to regain strength and movement in his arm. He picked up a Bible that a friend had given him.

As he read the Bible, he began to see God differently. Truth doused the angry fire in his heart.

"I always blamed God for anything that went wrong, but never gave Him credit for anything that was good," Vince says. At age eighteen, Vince decided it was time to get unstuck and move into a new season. He was invited to one of our New Life worship services. Vince slipped into the back of the auditorium having no idea what awaited him. I was speaking about how God became a man and though we have broken God's commandments and deserve the punishment for our actions, Jesus Christ gave His life to pay the penalty owed by all mankind.

I invited anyone who wanted prayer to come down to the front by the stage. Vince knew that he needed a new life and a fresh start. Slowly he walked to the very front of the auditorium. He knelt and prayed. God broke through all the built-up pain and anger. Something changed. He felt washed clean and alive.

The hand that had so often flipped God off now was lifted

in full surrender. The defiant arm had become the bullet-riddled arm. The crippled arm had become the miracle arm. And now that arm was extended in worship.

That day Vince stepped out of his cave of anger, hatred, and defiance. Vince went from being desperately stuck to stepping into a new season of his life. That severely scarred arm became the conversation piece that led to hundreds of conversations about God and His power to transform lives.

Two years ago Vince died of cancer. He left behind a wife and four children who loved him deeply. It had been two decades since he walked down that aisle to surrender his life. The day before Vince passed away, his hospital room was full of friends and family. He was thin and weak but he still raised his arm and prayed for each person in that room. Vince had definitely come out of his cave.

CROSSROAD

The time comes when a person needs to say goodbye to the safety of the cave and launch out into the risky world of faith living. Elijah's best days and most significant season of living were still ahead of him. He had to act decisively in the areas God had asked him to change. He managed to finish strong, complete his job, leave a legacy, and hand on the baton because he refused to stay in the cave.

You have a purpose and a unique calling. You may not fully understand it or be able to explain it yet, but you can discover it. And you must!

You may be looking out the oval-shaped opening to your

cave. You are beginning to see glimmers of visions and dreams. The possibility of a new season is opening before you. You have the opportunity to make your next season the best season of your life. You have a choice. You can stay in the comfort and relative security of your cave or you can choose to risk again. If you want to live, laugh, love, dream, and pursue your God-given call then you have but one choice.

It's time.

Take a deep breath.

Step out.

ACKNOWLEDGMENTS

There are some important people that I need to thank and acknowledge for their direct and indirect contributions to the content of this book.

Bob and Minnie Jobe, my parents, who left their country and friends to live on mission with God when I was just six months old. They taught me that life is an exciting adventure worth living for God.

My amazing wife, Dee. She has stood beside me, believed in my calling, and loved me for twenty-seven years of marriage. She has been encouraging me to write for years. Honey, I finally listened.

My kids, Marissa, Josiah, and Grant. You have been an inspiration to me in so many ways. I pray you never allow yourselves to get stuck for too long. I am grateful every day that God chose you to be my kids.

I appreciate the careful editing and insightful comments of Brandon O'Brien who, in the midst of relocating and starting a new job, took on this project. You have made this a better book.

To my incredible New Life friends and family. I feel loved, supported, and released to dream big when I am around you.

I am extremely grateful for the twenty-four New Life pastoral couples. Their friendship, passion, integrity, and tireless commitment to make a difference in the city of Chicago and beyond has inspired me.

Mike Berry, Luke Dudenhofer, and Chad Kimball for reading through these pages and offering good, practical insights. Moody Publishers, who believed I had something important to say. Greg Thornton, Duane Sherman, Betsey Newenhuyse, and the entire publishing team have encouraged me to take the time to write.

To many of you who have let me share your stories and shaped me through your lives and shared experiences.

Last, but certainly not least, I am very grateful for the more than 135 people who took a day to fast and pray during the seventy days that I was writing this book. They prayed and fasted for me and every future reader:

Linda Abdul, Chris Adams, Angelica Aguirre-Lozano, Eugene Alaniz, Lupe Alcazar, Sylvia Alonso, Laura Arroyo, Priscilla Avila, Yovani Bahena, Maria Baltazar, Mark Barlog, Cleo Bethea Jr., Phil Brayfield, Julio Caban, Reyna Cadena, Roger Cadena, Tony Caldaron, Marie Casica, Joan Castillo, Socorro Castro, Monica & Adrianna Ceballo, Adam Cervantes, Martha Contreras, Brandon Corbin, Jacob Corbin, Wiley Corbin, DelRosa Family, Charlene Dollinger, Trinidad Espinosa-Bahena, Marina & Julio Estrada, Camille Faust, Jim Faust, Diana Favela, Mike Feehan, Jorge Flores, Lily Flores, Oralia Forrester, Sarah Forrester, Reynaldo Fuentes, Manny Garcia, Dave Garratt, Diane Garratt, Alma Gomez, Michael Gonzalez, Vanessa Gonzalez,

Marisol Gordillo, Jose Guzman, Lorena Haro, Toni Holderbaum, Francisca Izguerra, Beata Jajesniak, Judy Kalina, Ken Kalina, Mimi Kedjareonkoon, Grace Koshy, Joe & Rhea Lopez, Michael Lopez, Veronica Lopez, Ileana Lopez-Gonzalez, Eric Lozano, Rebecca Luviano, Kate Martin, Jose A. Martinez, Leela Mathew, Eric McEvoy, Devene Mendiola, Louis Mercado, Sean Monahan, Lucas Monreal, Gabriel Montoya, Caterina Morales, Claudia Morales, Olivia Moren, Fernando & Maggie Moreno, Roy (Roel) Moya, Luis Olivera, Danny Ortiz, Laura Perez, Mario Perez, Rain Perez, Sarah Prosecky, Maria Del C. Quiles, Lucia Ramirez, Olga Ramirez, Sonia M. Ramirez, Dee Ramos, Tony Ramos, Araceli Renteria, Adriana Reyes, Irene Reyes, Marcos Rico, Theresa Rivera, Victor Rivera, Zulma Rivera, Claudia Rodarte, Adelina Rodriguez, Cassandra E. Rosario, Evelyn Rosario, Luis Rosario, Carmen Salgado, Gaby Salgado, Alejandra Sandoval, Maria Sarabia, Adriana Saucedo, Janet Saulter-Hemmer, Sandra Sheeha, Pat Sheehan, Salvador Tapia, Diane Tedesco, Faviola Torres, Elizabeth & Eugene Urbina, Aura Valdez, Elizabeth Valdez, Jose Valdez, Gloria Vargas, Irene Vasquez, Mike Vasquez, Genesi Vastarella, Lisette Vastarella, Laura Vazquez, Angela Vergara, Melissa Vergara, Lillybeth Vidal, Virginia Villalvazo, Fidelia Ybarra, Monica Zamora-Alamillo, Maria Zarowna, Dora Zaval, Karla Zavaleta, Mary Ziko.

ABOUT THE AUTHOR

Mark Jobe is an author, radio host, pastor, and social entrepreneur in the city of Chicago, the president of the Moody Bible Institute, and the founding pastor of New Life Community Church, which has grown from a handful to several thousand people currently meeting at over 25 locations throughout Chicagoland. Mark is also the founder of New Life Centers, an organization focused on helping and mentoring at-risk youth in the city and New Life Cities dedicated to planting churches in urban centers around the world. You can find more of Pastor Mark's teaching resources at www.pastormarkjobe.com. He holds a master's degree from Moody Theological Seminary and a doctorate degree from Bakke Graduate University.

For more information visit these sites:
New Life Community Church, www.newlifechicago.org
New Life Centers, www.newlifecenters.org
New Life Cities, www.newlifecities.org
Chicago Office: 773-838-9470

NOTES

Introduction

1. Nicholas White in Rich McHugh and Jonann Brady, "Man Trapped in Elevator for 41 Hours," *ABCNews.com*, April 21, 2008, http://abcnews.go.com/GMA/story?id=4693690

2. Troy Fredrickson in Amy Macavinta, "Fireman's close call underscores danger of carbon monoxide, need for detectors," *HJNews.com*, January 8, 2012, http://news.hjnews.com/news/article_0f2b6676-39bd-11e1-9f8a-001871e3ce6c.html?mode=jqm.

Chapter Two: We All Get Stuck Sometime

1. Robert L. Deffinbaugh, "The Life and Times of Elijah the Prophet—Elijah Throws in the Towel (1 Kings 18:45–19:21)," *Bible.org*, August 24, 2004, https://bible.org/seriespage/life-and-times-elijah-prophet%E2%80%94-elijah-throws-towel-1-kings-1845-1921.

2. See Bryant G. Wood, "What Do Mt. Horeb, the Mountain of God, Mt. Paran, and Mt. Seir Have to Do with Mt. Sinai?" *Associates for Biblical Research*, November 17, 2008, https://www.biblearchaeology.org/post/2008/11/what-do-mt-horeb2c-the-mountain-of-god2c-mt-paran-and-mt-seir-have-to-do-with-mt-sinai.aspx#Article.

Chapter Four: Break Out of Isolation

1. Robert D. Putnam, *Bowling Alone: The Collapse and Revival of American Community* (New York: Simon & Schuster; 2000), Kindle.

2. This study has often been cited in speeches, blogs, sermons, and other sources and is widely available on the Internet.

3. *John Lanferman Blog.* http://johnlanferman.blogspot.com/2011/08/lonely-people-designed-for-community.html.

4. Ibid.

5. Wayne Cordeiro, *Leading on Empty: Refilling Your Tank and Renewing Your Passion* (Ada, MI: Bethany House, 2010), 95.

6. Hara Estroff Marano, "What Is Solitude?" *Psychology Today*, November 21, 2013, http://www.psychologytoday.com/articles/200308/what-is-solitude.

7. That is the finding of a new survey by LifeWay Research of 1,000 American Protestant pastors; see http://www.lifeway.com/Article/Research-Survey-Pastors-feel-privileged-and-positive-though-discouragement-can-come.

8. Henry Cloud, *Boundaries for Leaders: Results, Relationships, and Being Ridiculously in Charge* (New York: HarperBusiness, 2013), 199.

Chapter Six: Turn Up the God Volume

1. www.ohranger.com/mammoth-cave/earthquakes.
2. Charles Spurgeon, "The Still Small Voice," delivered July 9, 1882, http://www.ccel.org/ccel/spurgeon/sermons28.xxxii.html.
3. Henry Cloud, *Boundaries for Leaders: Results, Relationships, and Being Ridiculously in Charge* (New York City: Harper Business, 2013), Kindle.
4. Brother Lawrence, *The Practice of the Presence of God* (Radford, VA: Wilder Publications, 2008), 39–40.

Chapter Seven: Reenvision Your Life Story

1. Francis Chan, *Crazy Love* (Colorado Springs: David C Cook, 2008), 24.
2. William Booth, *The General's Letters, 1885* (London: Salvation Army, 1890), 4–5.
3. A. W. Tozer, *The Knowledge of the Holy* (North Charleston, SC: Independent Publishing Platform, 2013), 8.

Chapter Ten: Take the First Step

1. Dr. Ralph F. Wilson, "Healing the Woman with a Bent Back," http://www.jesuswalk.com/lessons/13_10-17.htm.

Chapter Twelve: Breathe the Air of a New Season

1. www.nytimes.com/2010/12/06/world/europe/06spain.html?_r=0.
2. Patrick Lencioni, *The Advantage: Why Organizational Health Trumps Everything Else In Business* (San Francisco: Jossey-Bass, 2012), 7.
3. *The New York Times*, "The Dot-Com Bubble Bursts," December 24, 2000, www.nytimes.com/2000/12/24/opinion/the-dot-com-bubble-bursts.html.

FREE RESOURCES ONLINE:

NewLifeChicago.org

Go to **https://getunstuck-book.com** and begin using tools to equip you, your small group, and your church to move out of their cave and into their call.

Pastor Mark Jobe and New Life Community Church have created FREE resources for you:

- Study Guide
- Videos
- And More

SPIRITUAL LEADERSHIP

ISBN: 978-0-8024-1670-4

With more than one million copies in print, *Spiritual Leadership* stands as a proven classic for developing such leadership. In these pages J. Oswald Sanders presents the key principles of leadership in both the temporal and spiritual realms, illustrating his points with examples from Scripture and biographies of eminent men of God (Moses, Nehemiah, Paul, David Livingstone, Charles Spurgeon, and others).

also available as an ebook

Find it at your favorite local or online bookstore.

D. L. Moody — A Life

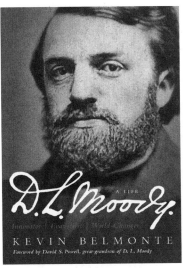

ISBN: 978-0-8024-1204-1

A sterling philanthropist and educator, D. L. Moody was also the finest evangelist in the nineteenth century—bringing the transformative message of the gospel before 100 million people on both sides of the Atlantic in an age long before radio and television. Thousands of underprivileged young people were educated in the schools he established. Before the Civil War, he went to a place no one else would: the slums of Chicago called Little Hell. The mission he started there, in an abandoned saloon, over time drew hundreds of children and prompted a visit from president-elect, Abraham Lincoln in 1860.

also available as an ebook

Find it at your favorite local or online bookstore.

Straight *talk*

PASTOR MARK JOBE

Straight to the heart
Straight to the point

WMBI FM 90.1

Also available at
straighttalkchicago.com